COMPREHENSIVE RESEARCH
AND STUDY GUIDE

Elizabeth Bishop

BLOOM'S
MAJOR
POETS

EDITED AND WITH AN INTRODUCTION
BY HAROLD BLOOM

CURRENTLY AVAILABLE

BLOOM'S MAJOR DRAMATISTS	BLOOM'S MAJOR NOVELISTS	BLOOM'S MAJOR POETS	BLOOM'S MAJOR SHORT STORY WRITERS
Aeschylus	Jane Austen	Maya Angelou	Jorge Louis Borges
Aristophanes	The Brontës	Elizabeth Bishop	Italo Calvino
Bertold Brecht	Willa Cather	William Blake	Raymond Carver
Anton Chekhov	Stephen Crane	Gwendolyn Brooks	Anton Chekhov
Henrik Ibsen	Charles Dickens	Robert Browning	Joseph Conrad
Ben Johnson	William Faulkner	Geoffrey Chaucer	Stephen Crane
Christopher Marlowe	F. Scott Fitzgerald	Sameul Taylor Coleridge	William Faulkner
Arthur Miller	Nathaniel Hawthorne	Dante	F. Scott Fitzgerald
Eugene O'Neill	Ernest Hemingway	Emily Dickinson	Nathaniel Hawthorne
Shakespeare's Comedies	Henry James	John Donne	Ernest Hemingway
Shakespeare's Histories	James Joyce	H.D.	O. Henry
Shakespeare's Romances	D. H. Lawrence	T. S. Eliot	Shirley Jackson
Shakespeare's Tragedies	Toni Morrison	Robert Frost	Henry James
George Bernard Shaw	John Steinbeck	Seamus Heaney	James Joyce
Neil Simon	Stendhal	Homer	Franz Kafka
Oscar Wilde	Leo Tolstoy	Langston Hughes	D.H. Lawrence
Tennessee Williams	Mark Twain	John Keats	Jack London
August Wilson	Alice Walker	John Milton	Thomas Mann
	Edith Wharton	Sylvia Plath	Herman Melville
	Virginia Woolf	Edgar Allan Poe	Flannery O'Connor
		Poets of World War I	Edgar Allan Poe
		Shakespeare's Poems & Sonnets	Katherine Anne Porter
		Percy Shelley	J. D. Salinger
		Alfred, Lord Tennyson	John Steinbeck
		Walt Whitman	Mark Twain
		William Carlos Williams	John Updike
		William Wordsworth	Eudora Welty
		William Butler Yeats	

COMPREHENSIVE RESEARCH
AND STUDY GUIDE

Elizabeth
Bishop

BLOOM'S
MAJOR
POETS

EDITED AND WITH AN INTRODUCTION
BY HAROLD BLOOM

811.54
ELI

First Printing
1 3 5 7 9 8 6 4 2

Library of Congress Cataloging-in-Publication Data
Elizabeth Bishop / Harold Bloom, ed.
        p. cm. —(Bloom's major poets)
Includes bibliographical references and index.
    ISBN 0-7910-6813-7
    1. Bishop, Elizabeth, 1911–1979—Criticism and interpretation. 2.
Women and literature—United States—History—20th century. I. Bloom,
Harold. II. Series.
    PS3503 .I785 2002
    811'.54—dc21   2002002774

Chelsea House Publishers
1974 Sproul Road, Suite 400
Broomall, PA 19008-0914

The Chelsea House World Wide Web address is http://www.chelseahouse.com

Contributing Editor: Jesse Zuba

Layout by EJB Publishing Services

CONTENTS

USER'S GUIDE

This volume is designed to present biographical, critical, and bibliographical information on the author and the author's best-known or most important poems. Following Harold Bloom's editor's note and introduction is a concise biography of the author that discusses major life events and important literary accomplishments. A critical analysis of each poem follows, tracing significant themes, patterns, and motifs in the work. As with any study guide, it is recommended that the reader read the poem beforehand and have a copy of the poem being discussed available for quick reference.

A selection of critical extracts, derived from previously published material, follows each thematic analysis. In most cases, these extracts represent the best analysis available from a number of leading critics. Because these extracts are derived from previously published material, they will include the original notations and references when available. Each extract is cited, and readers are encouraged to check the original publication as they continue their research. A bibliography of the author's writings, a list of additional books and articles on the author and their work, and an index of themes and ideas conclude the volume.

ABOUT THE EDITOR

Harold Bloom is Sterling Professor of the Humanities at Yale University and Henry W. and Albert A. Berg Professor of English at the New York University Graduate School. He is the author of over 20 books, and the editor of more than 30 anthologies of literary criticism.

Professor Bloom's works include *Shelly's Mythmaking* (1959), *The Visionary Company* (1961), *Blake's Apocalypse* (1963), *Yeats* (1970), *A Map of Misreading* (1975), *Kabbalah and Criticism* (1975), *Agon: Toward a Theory of Revisionism* (1982), *The American Religion* (1992), *The Western Canon* (1994), and *Omens of Millennium: The Gnosis of Angels, Dreams, and Resurrection* (1996). *The Anxiety of Influence* (1973) sets forth Professor Bloom's provocative theory of the literary relationships between the great writers and their predecessors. His most recent books include *Shakespeare: The Invention of the Human*, a 1998 National Book Award finalist, *How to Read and Why* (2000), and *Stories and Poems for Extremely Intelligent Children of All Ages* (2001).

Professor Bloom earned his Ph.D. from Yale University in 1955 and has served on the Yale faculty since then. He is a 1985 MacArthur Foundation Award recipient and served as the Charles Eliot Norton Professor of Poetry at Harvard University in 1987–88. In 1999 he was awarded the prestigious American Academy of Arts and Letters Gold Medal for Criticism. Professor Bloom is the editor of several other Chelsea House series in literary criticism, including BLOOM'S MAJOR SHORT STORY WRITERS, BLOOM'S MAJOR NOVELISTS, BLOOM'S MAJOR DRAMATISTS, MODERN CRITICAL INTERPRETATIONS, MODERN CRITICAL VIEWS, and BLOOM'S BIOCRITIQUES.

EDITOR'S NOTE

My Introduction centers upon Elizabeth Bishop's relationship to an American tradition in poetry that includes Emily Dickinson, Wallace Stevens and Marianne Moore, with particular reference to "At The Fishhouses" and "The End of March."

"The Monument," which is Bishop's "Kublai Khan," as Bonnie Costello accurately notes, is read by Costello as a "dialogue of art," while the Irish poet Seamus Heaney admires Bishop's mastery in it. Marilyn May Lombardi reads "The Monument" as a critique of Wallace Stevens, who nevertheless contaminates the poem. Bishop's self-trust is persuasively noted and commended by David Bromwich.

"Roosters" is introduced by Bishop's remarks on "the essential baseness of militarism" in a letter to Marianne Moore, after which Loiuis Bogan reviews *North and South*, the collection countaining "Roosters." The baseness Bishop mentions is explored in observations by Willard Spiegelman and Victoria Harrison. James Longenbach rather desperately quests to impart politics to the apolitical Bishop, after which David Bromwich compares Bishop to Moore on the basis of "Roosters."

"At the Fishhouses" is read by David Kalstone in relation both to Wordsworth and Stevens, and by Elizabeth Spires as a peculiar act of knowledge. Robert Dale Parker meditates upon the image of the sea in the poem, after which Bonnie Costello sees Bishop as revising the Romantic crisis lyric, and Anne Colwell finds in "At the Fishhouses" a profound mediation of experience.

"Crusoe in England," a superb dramatic monologue, is introduced by Bishop's letter to James Merrill in which she restores some lines to Crusoe's remarks on Friday. Helen Vendler sees love escaping language in the poem, while Joanne Feit Diehl muses on Bishop's relationship to Emerson's American Sublime. Bishop's departures from Daniel Defoe are examined by Steven Hamelman, after which C. K. Doreski meditates upon the Crusoe-Friday friendship in Bishop, and Susan McCabe traces elements of the poet's own biography in Crusoe's monologue.

"The End of March" is introduced by Bishop's remarks on the surrealism of everyday life. The poem's prosody is analyzed by

Penelope Laurans, after which Sherod Santos commends Bishop's aesthetic patience, and Lorrie Goldensohn invokes other renunciations of retirement-fantasies in Bishop. John Hollander powerfully evokes the context of *Geography III*, as a book, while Langdon Hammer defines some of the differences between Bishop's modes of expression in letters and poems.

Harold Bloom

In her early poem "The Unbeliever," Elizabeth Bishop juxtaposed three poets (as I allegorize it) or else kinds of poets, in the figures of cloud, seagull, and unbeliever. The cloud is introspective, or even solipsistic: a William Wordsworth or Wallace Stevens. The gull is a visionary in a tower: a Shelley or Hart Crane. The unbeliever, dreaming catastrophe, is an Emily Dickinson or Elizabeth Bishop. Where Stevens or Crane asserts the power of the poet's mind over the sea or universe of death, Bishop observes the sea accurately in her dream:

> which was, "I must not fall.
> The spangled sea below wants me to fall.
> It is hard as diamonds; it wants to destroy us all."

Though she stemmed from Wordsworth and Stevens as well as from Dickinson and Marianne Moore, Elizabeth Bishop shied away from celebrating the powers of poetry, which she judged sublimely "useless." One suspects she meant "useless" as Oscar Wilde meant it: to be free of moralizing purposes.

Bishop is one of the major American poets, the peer of Whitman and Dickinson, Frost and Stevens, Eliot and Hart Crane. She is so meticulous and so original that she tends to be both under-read and rather weakly misread. Most frequently she is praised for her "eye," as though she were a master of optics. But her actual achievement is to see what cannot quite be seen, and to say what cannot quite be said.

The influence of Wallace Stevens upon her work rendered Bishop rather uneasy, and she would like to have been considered a disciple of Marianne Moore, her friend and mentor. But poets are chosen *by* their precursors: they do not choose. Stevens's greatest poetry gives us what he called: "the hum of thoughts evaded in the mind," and so does Bishop's. Moore, endlessly curious about *things*, created a mosaic of impressions, brilliantly vivid. With Stevens and Bishop, we are in a cosmos of imagined things, things taken up into the mind. Stevens's massive aesthetic broodings are scaled down and somewhat ironized in Bishop, but her mode of reflection essentially is his. And her sense of the poet's predicament is also his: that we live in a place that is not our own, and much more, not ourselves.

"At the Fishhouses" is Bishop at her most memorable, no longer an unbeliever but "a believer in total immersion." Like Wordsworth returning to Tintern Abbey, there to exchange experiential loss for imaginative gain, Bishop goes back to Nova Scotia, where she had lived for a time in childhood, with her maternal grandparents. The long, first verse paragraph is held together by an imagery of gloaming: "All is silver." An "apparent translucence" is enhanced by the iridescence of the remnants of fish, its "the sparse bright sprinkle" of the grass, and sequin-like fish scales that adhere to the old fisherman, a friend of Bishop's late grandfather.

A brief, six-line transitional section takes us from "thin silver/tree trunks" to the gray stones in the water. In the long third verse-paragraph, we move from the "all is silver" vision to the grayness of stone and icy water. If the silver is the emblem of experiential loss, then the gray ambivalently suggests an imaginative gain that is dangerous and potentially hurtful: water and stones burn with "a dark gray flame":

> It is like what we imagine knowledge to be:
> dark, salt, clear, moving, utterly free,
> drawn from the cold hard mouth
> of the world, derived from the rocky breasts
> forever, flowing and drawn, and since
> our knowledge is historical, flowing, and flown.

Translucence is lost, and no present knowing is gained in its place. Yet the utter freedom of that "flowing, and flown," has to be an imaginative value, an achievement of a fully articulated poem.

"The End of March," which I think is Bishop's supreme poem, culminates on a wonderful trope of "the lion sun," Stevensian but turned against Stevens's figure of thought. In Stevens, the lion is emblematic of poetry as a destructive force, or again of the poet imposing the power of his mind over the universe of death. The great culmination of this figure is in *An Ordinary Evening in New Haven*:

> Say of each lion of the spirit

> It is a cat if a sleek transparency
> That shines with a nocturnal shine alone.
> The great cat must stand potent in the sun.

That lion sun is Whitmanian: it represents an American Sublime. Affectionately, Bishop answers Stevens with a playful difference, more like Dickinson or Moore than like Whitman:

> They could have been teasing the lion sun,
> except that now he was behind them
> a sun who'd walked the beach the last low tide,
> making those big, majestic paw-prints,
> who perhaps had batted a kite out of the sky to play with.

This lion sun is poetry as a playful force, and not a destructive one. Bishop's wit, never more playful, is never more luminous. To the stark shore-odes of Whitman and of Stevens she has added a postlude, as memorable in its mode, as Whitman and Stevens were in theirs.

Elizabeth Bishop

Elizabeth Bishop was born on February 9, 1911 in Worcester, Massachusetts, the only child of William Thomas Bishop, a vice president in his father's construction company, and Gertrude (Bulmer) Bishop. Her parents' marriage lasted just three years, cut short by her father's death from kidney disease when Elizabeth was only eight months old. His death aggravated her mother's already unstable mental health, and after several breakdowns she entered a Massachusetts hospital, removing later to an asylum in Canada, where she died in 1934. Following her mother's admittance, Elizabeth, who was never again to see her mother, lived with her maternal grandparents in Great Village, Nova Scotia for a short time before being taken to live in Worcester with her father's parents so she could attend school in the United States. In 1918 she moved yet again, this time to live with her aunt and uncle outside of Boston, and though her fourth childhood home proved a positive, stable environment, her frail health kept her from going to school regularly until she was sixteen. Her condition left her with plenty of time to read, however, and by the time she entered Walnut Hill School in 1927 she had already become familiar with the poetry of Walt Whitman and Gerard Manley Hopkins, among others. She continued to explore literature during her high school years, going through "a Shelley phase, a Browning phase, and a brief Swinburne phase," as she related in an interview, and she published several early works in the school's literary magazine.

In 1930 Bishop went to Vassar College, where she took a B.A. in English in 1934. Among her classmates were Mary McCarthy, Eleanor Clark, and Muriel Rukeyser, each of whom were soon to begin prominent literary careers of their own, and the four of them started a literary journal entitled *The Conspirito*. Her literary career began in earnest while she was still an undergraduate, as Bishop's poems and short stories were accepted not only by the college review but by national magazines. Though she had originally intended to pursue a career in medicine, by the time she graduated she had determined to move to New York City to work as a writer—a change stimulated in large part by her new friendship with Marianne Moore, who mentored Bishop in the years that followed their 1934 meeting. After leaving Vassar Bishop began the travels that were to leave such a large impression on her work, spending time in England, France, North Africa, Spain, and Italy before settling in Key West, Florida in 1938. She published poems in the *Partisan Review*, *Poetry*, and *The New Yorker*, and other prestigious periodicals during the 1930's and early 1940's, but it was not until 1946 that she published her first collection, *North and South*, as the winner of the Houghton Mifflin poetry competition. Her debut volume was very well-received: Randall Jarrell compared it to recent books by William Carlos Williams and Robert Graves, and Marianne Moore hailed her as "someone who knows, who is not didactic." A decade in the making, *North and South* collects some of Bishop's best-known poems, including "The Monument," "Roosters," "The Imaginary Iceberg," and the perennial favorite of anthologists, "The Fish." The book established Bishop's reputation for nuanced description, emotional reticence, and themes of travel, and on the strength of its success she won a Guggenheim Fellowship in 1947 and was appointed Consultant in Poetry at the Library of Congress in 1949.

In November of 1951 Bishop began a voyage around South America; when the trip was interrupted by an illness, however, she decided to remain in Brazil, where she lived with her companion Lota Ostellat de Macedo Soares in Rio de Janeiro for the next fifteen years. Relentlessly self-critical, Bishop's high standards and painstaking habits of revision ensured a slow progress toward her next book-length publication, which did not appear until 1955. Her publishers augmented the new collection by reprinting it together with her previous volume as *Poems: North and South—A Cold Spring*. Among the eighteen new poems featured in the book were several that rank as masterpieces, including "At the Fishhouses," "The Bight," and "Over 2,000 Illustrations and a Complete Concordance." The book won the Pulitzer Prize for poetry in 1956. Bishop's third book, *Questions of Travel*, appeared in 1965. The collection is divided into subsections entitled "Brazil" and "Elsewhere," an arrangement that places her continuing interest in her past alongside her explorations of the history, culture, and landscape of Brazil. "In the Village," a short story about her mother's collapse that had appeared in *The New Yorker*, was also included in *Questions of Travel*, largely at the behest of Robert Lowell, who had published an autobiographical prose-piece of his own in his influential 1959 collection *Life Studies*. The book showcases Bishop's formal dexterity as it ranges from ballad meter in "The Burglar of Babylon" to the recycled end-words of "Sestina," titled after the difficult lyric form it embodies. The collection garnered rave reviews, particularly from fellow poets, and was followed in 1969 by a collected edition of her work, which won the National Book Award.

In the late sixties Bishop's personal life took a downward turn. The object along with Lota Soares of criticism from the Brazilian press, Bishop's distress was exacerbated by illness and compounded with relationship troubles. She left Brazil to teach at the University of Washington in 1966. Soares committed suicide the following year, shortly after joining Bishop during what was intended to be a long visit to New York. The poet spent a year in San Francisco before going back to Brazil, where she remained until 1969, when she returned to the United States to teach at Harvard.

Bishop conducted writing seminars regularly at Harvard until 1977, and taught for one more semester at New York University before retiring from academia. Her final volume, *Geography III*, appeared in 1976 and reconfirmed her stature as one of the finest American poets of her generation. She received the National Book Critics' Circle Award for the collection, which featured her acclaimed dramatic monologue "Crusoe in England," as well as the frequently anthologized villanelle "One Art," and "The End of March." Bishop died on October 6, 1979.

CRITICAL ANALYSIS OF

"The Monument"

"The Monument" is an ecphrastic poem that presents a dialogue between a pair of observers—one a sort of spokesperson for the monument whose grave description and reservedly appreciative attitude suggest a caricature of a curator, and the other a skeptic whose persistent questions and impatience mark her as a bored museumgoer. Together they regard a monument made of stacked wooden boxes set against a background of sea and sky which are also of wood—a medium that points to the poem's source in Bishop's fascination with a technique of taking rubbings from the grain of wood called *frottage*, and more particularly with Max Ernst's "False Positions," a surrealist *frottage* depicting a pair of long, vertical cylinders standing on a horizontal base. The dialogic structure of the poem exemplifies its resistance to thematic closure. The poem explores questions about art, immortality, history, memory, and perception, primarily by multiplying possible answers. It ends not by defining the significance of the monument, but by introducing an explicitly self-referential dimension to the poem—the monument is "the beginning" of a "poem, or monument," among other possibilities—that works to further this process of proliferation. The poem's final sentence reflects its concerns both with resisting closure and with the aesthetic by recommending a continued attentiveness: "Watch it closely."

The opening lines practice what the poem preaches in its last sentence by parading a capacity for close observation, where the closeness registers in the speaker's patient re-phrasings and qualifications: "Now can you see the monument? It is of wood/built somewhat like a box. No. Built/like several boxes in descending sizes/one above the other." The care the speaker takes to word her account accurately exemplifies Bishop's characteristic interest in descriptive fidelity. Also audible through the speaker's adjustments of phrasing is an interest in anticipating and pre-empting any complaints her fellow observer might be inclined to make. This anxiety is reflected in the speaker's qualifications: a "sort of" fleur-de-lys adorns the top of the monument; the jig-saw work is "vaguely whittled." A pair of par-

17

enthetical asides, in which the speaker endeavors to contextualize her meaning with examples and to clarify it by putting it another way, respectively, reinforce this pattern still further. The sheer extensiveness of the speaker's opening description and her interlocutor's plaintive bewilderment lend their exchange, as David Bromwich notes, the accents of farce. Also, the pattern of qualification points up a tension between visual and verbal modes of representation: the poem can present the picture, but not completely, and it admits its inadequacy in this regard by obsessively second-guessing its own rhetoric.

Perspective remains vexed throughout the poem; it is a problem to which the interruptions of the second speaker give a voice even as they further complicate it. That the "view is geared" so "low" that "there is no 'far away'" suggests that the monument is portrayed without a foreground, against a flat backdrop—one third sea and two-thirds sky—that undoes the illusions of depth and distance. Strangely though, "we are far away within the view," a condition that seems paradoxical but that points to the idea that the speaker is imagining how "we" must look "within the view" possible from atop the monument. It is the possibility of being viewed from "within the view" that sponsors the listener's sudden concern for establishing his own location: "Where are we? Are we in Asia Minor/or in Mongolia?" The range of possibilities evoked by the question reflects a sense of radical disorientation, and his wonder as to why "that strange sea make[s] no sound" furthers this sense of estrangement by unsettling the very status of the monument. If what they regard is a picture of a monument, why would the sea in the backdrop be expected to make a sound? If the sea consists of "horizontal boards," which suggest they are viewing a work of art, why is their own location in question? Later the interlocutor complains of being "tired of breathing this eroded air,/this dryness in which the monument is cracking," as if the observers shared the atmosphere of the monument, even though its sky "is palings," its sunlight "splintery," and its clouds "long-fibred."

The poem refuses to resolve these ambiguities of orientation and perspective, a refusal embodied in the speaker's response to her fellow observer's questions. Instead of defining their location or speculating on the soundless sea in the background of the monument, she sketches in a possible past for what they see: "An ancient promontory, an ancient principality whose artist-prince might have wanted/to mark a tomb or boundary, or make/a melancholy or romantic scene of it." The monument "marks" time by functioning as a sort of memorial, even as its "warped" decorations and "weathered" appearance attest to its subjection to time. Too, it is a work of art, erected by an "artist-prince" who may have intended to make the scene it inhabits seem "melancholy or romantic." Nature and art merge with and unsettle one another in the exchange that follows the initial interruption, much as the viewers' perspective merges with and is unsettled by the imagined perspective possible from the monument's heights.

The continued interruptions of the second speaker center on the issue of art's subjection to nature and spur the defender's commentary on the value of art. The skeptical second speaker's observations de-idealize art by calling attention to the way in which the medium—wood—shows through the scene portrayed, revealing its status as illusion, and by noting its inability to withstand "the conditions of its existence." These opinions go uncontroverted in the poem, which, as Bonnie Costello suggests, "eschews the idea of mastery or transcendence" of the flux of nature. But the skeptical observer's final questions—"Why did you bring me here to see it?/A temple of crates in cramped and crated scenery,/what can it prove?"—prompt a defense of the value of art. That it "chose that way to grow and not to move" suggests that the monument ought to be considered on its own terms, not asked to be something other than itself. And yet the virtues and purposes of the monument—it has life, wishes, cherishes, commemorates, shelters "what is within"—suggest an intimate relation between this "object," its audience, and the artist-prince who commissioned it. The last speech calls attention particularly to the inscrutability and opacity of the monument: it may or may not be hollow and may or may not house the artist-prince's bones. But the comparison of the monument to the "beginning" of several kinds of art, "all of wood," bespeaks a potential for a continuing evolution of the relation between the artist, artwork, and audience, predicated upon the disciplined attention the poem counsels as it closes.

CRITICAL VIEWS ON

"The Monument"

ROBERT LOWELL REVIEWS *NORTH AND SOUTH*

[Robert Lowell (1917–1977), perhaps the most influential poet of his generation, gave rise to Confessional verse with his book *Life Studies* (1959). His other collections of poetry include *For the Union Dead* (1964), *Near the Ocean* (1967), and *Lord Wear's Castle* (1946), which won the Pulitzer Prize. In this excerpt from a review of *North and South*, Lowell, who was to become Bishop's close friend, describes the symbolic and rhetorical patterns that many of her early poems share, and goes on to locate Bishop within the context of modernism, comparing her work to that of Kafka, Frost, Williams, and Moore.]

On the surface, her poems are observations—surpassingly accurate, witty and well-arranged, but nothing more. Sometimes she writes of a place where she has lived on the Atlantic Coast; at others, of a dream, a picture, or some fantastic object. One is reminded of Kafka and certain abstract paintings, and is left rather at sea about the actual subjects of the poems. I think that at least nine-tenths of them fall into a single symbolic pattern. Characterizing it is an elusive business.

There are two opposing factors, the first is something in motion, weary but persisting, almost always failing and on the point of disintegrating, and yet, for the most part, stoically maintained. This is morality, memory, the weed that grows to divide, and the dawn that advances, illuminates and calls to work, the monument "that wants to be a monument," the waves rolling in on the shore, breaking, and being replaced, the echo of the hermit's voice saying, "love must be put in action"; it is the stolid little mechanical horse that carries a dancer, and all those things of memory that "cannot forget us half so easily as they can forget themselves." The second factor is a terminus: rest, sleep, fulfillment or death. This is the imaginary iceberg, the moon which the Man-moth thinks is a small clean hole through which he must thrust his head; it is sleeping on the top of a mast, and the peaceful ceiling: "But oh, that we could sleep up there."

The motion-process is usually accepted as necessary and, therefore, good; yet it is dreary and exhausting. But the formula is mysterious and gently varies with its objects. The terminus is sometimes pathetically or humorously desired as a letting-go or annihilation; sometimes it is fulfillment and the complete harmonious exercise of one's faculties. The rainbow of spiritual peace seen as the author decides to let a fish go, is both like and unlike the moon which the Man-moth mistakes for an opening. In "Large Bad Picture," ships are at anchor in a northern bay, and the author reflects, "It would be hard to say what brought them there/Commerce or contemplation." The structure of a Bishop poem is simple and effective. It will usually start as description or descriptive narrative, then either the poet or one of her characters or objects reflects. The tone of these reflections is pathetic, witty, fantastic, or shrewd. Frequently, it is all these things at once. Its purpose is to heighten and dramatize the description and, at the same time, to unify and universalize it. In this, and in her marvelous command of shifting speech-tones, Bishop resembles Robert Frost.

In her bare objective language, she also reminds one at times of William Carlos Williams; but it is obvious that her most important model is Marianne Moore. Her dependence should not be defined as imitation, but as one of development and transformation. (. . .)

Although Bishop would be unimaginable without Moore, her poems add something to the original, and are quite as genuine. Both poets use an elaborate descriptive technique, love exotic objects, are moral, genteel, witty, and withdrawn. There are metrical similarities, and a few of Bishop's poems are done in Moore's manner. But the differences in method and personality are great. Bishop is usually present in her poems; they happen to her, she speaks, and often centers them on herself. Others are dramatic and have human actors. She uses dreams and allegories. (Like Kafka's, her treatment of the absurd is humorous, matter of fact, and logical.) She hardly ever quotes from other writers. Most of her meters are accentual-syllabic. Compared with Moore, she is softer, dreamier, more human and more personal; she is less idiosyncratic, and less magnificent. She is probably slighter; of course, being much younger, she does not have nearly so many extraordinarily good poems.

—Robert Lowell, *Sewanee Review* 55 (Summer 1947): pp. 497–499. Reprinted in *Elizabeth Bishop and Her Art*, ed. Lloyd Schwartz and Sybil P. Estess (Ann Arbor: University of Michigan Press, 1983): pp. 186–188.

BONNIE COSTELLO ON THE FUNCTION OF ART IN THE POEM

[Bonnie Costello writes frequently on contemporary poetry and teaches at Boston University. Her books include *Marianne Moore: Imaginary Possessions* (1981) and *Elizabeth Bishop: Questions of Mastery* (1988), from which the extract that follows is drawn. Costello suggests that Bishop's poem offers a uniquely modest perspective on the function of art, in contrast to a Romantic tradition of monument poems in which art is represented as a refuge from time.]

"The Monument" (CP, 23–25) stresses this value of commemoration over transport. Bishop again explores the paradox between art's crude means and the affective power of its illusions. The poet shapes the opposition as a dialogue, in which one speaker finds only "piled-up boxes," the other "a monument." The defender of the monument gets the final word, finding a role for art which is preservative and commemorative but not nostalgic. Art acts and exists for this speaker within history rather than above or beyond in a space of mastery. The poem also implicitly reflects the relation of words and images, the one interpreting and extending the other. More directly allusive than most of Bishop's poetry, "The Monument" addresses a long tradition of poems about monument making, which includes Coleridge's "Kubla Khan," Shelley's "Ozymandias," Yeats's "Sailing to Byzantium," and Stevens' "Anecdote of the Jar" (itself allusive of Keats's "Ode on a Grecian Urn"). Her version of the monument is particularly suited to a modern age, preserving a place for art after dismantling its idealism.

Bishop's "The Monument" compares most directly to Coleridge's "Kubla Khan," a dream of artistic mastery over nature's laws. Like Khan, Bishop's artist is a prince, a figure of authority, but his decree admits the "conditions of its existence." He is more obscure and less presumptuous than Khan. The poet conjectures that the "artist-prince / might have wanted to build a monument / to mark a tomb or boundary, or make / a melancholy or romantic scene of it. . . . " These are modest purposes: to commemorate, designate, evoke. History has erased his intention. The sea surrounding this monument is not defiantly sunless like Coleridge's, but rather is made of drift-wood, already overexposed to the elements.

The monument does not make the past present; it merely stands as a sign of the past. "The bones of the artist-prince may be inside / or far away on even drier soil." Either way Bishop offers no illusions about immortality through art. She does not dictate despair, however, any more than she dictates reliquary worship. "But roughly but adequately it can shelter / what is within (which after all / cannot have been intended to be seen)." The syntactic and descriptive evasion of "what is within" reminds us that this subjective center can only be hypothetical. The recognition of expressive intention within the artifact is essential to its function, however. "Do you see nothing there?" asks Hamlet about the ghost of his father. "Nothing at all, yet all there is I see," replies the Queen. Such is the dialogue of art in this poem. Art exists in a process, to which certain attitudes are preliminary: "Now can you see the monument?" It is the seeing-in or seeing-as which transforms art from mere thing to monument; "what is within" can only be inferred. Perhaps "what is within" is simply the potential to commemorate, which is not really "within" at all. The monument exemplifies the artichoke-like unfolding of the life of a work, its making, its beholding, and its history. The decaying monument simply acknowledges a boundary to human aspiration. Its inscription does not seek to aggrandize as Ozymandias had ("Look on my Works, ye Mighty and despair!"), or to mystify in Keatsian tautology ("Beauty is truth, truth beauty,") but merely to cherish and commemorate.

—Bonnie Costello, *Elizabeth Bishop: Questions of Mastery* (Cambridge: Harvard University Press, 1991): pp. 218–219.

[Nobel Prize-winning poet Seamus Heaney teaches at Harvard University and has published ten collections of verse, including *Death of a Naturalist* (1966), *Field Work* (1979), and *Seeing Things* (1991), as well as several book-length translations and criticisms. In the following extract Heaney describes the subtle relation between Bishop's reticence and the intensity of her descriptive fidelity.]

'Sestina', with its inscrutable house, performs the same reflexive but ultimately salubrious function as the monument performs in an early Bishop poem called (with equal plainness) 'The Monument'. This monument is made of wood, of boxes placed upon boxes; like the sestina it is both enigmatic and entirely satisfactory. It promises nothing beyond what it exhibits, and yet it seems to be standing over something which it also stands *for*. Once again, a withdrawn pressure, an inscrutable purpose or missing element is what the resulting structure exists to express or shelter. In fact, the final lines of the poem declare that the monument commemorates something undeclared, something embodying and maintaining a meaning it feels no need to proclaim: (. . .)

This monument to something which 'cannot have been intended to be seen' finds itself menaced by the very light which goes around it 'like a prowling animal'. Yet in spite of the guardedness which these conditions induce, it still does want 'to cherish something'. And if we watch it closely, as we are counselled to, we shall find that in being an object which has life and 'can shelter / what is within', it resembles the work of the poet who imagined it into being in the first place. For the gratifying thing about Elizabeth Bishop's poetry is that in the end it too overcomes the guardedness of its approach. It may be an observant poetry but it does not finally, in the colloquial sense of the term, 'watch it', even though the inclination to caution is persistently felt as a condition of the poet's style. Qualification is her natural habit of mind, but even so, the poetry continually manages to go out to greet what is there, to salute what Louis MacNeice called 'the drunkenness of things being various'. And it justifies itself *as* poetry by the thoroughness of its assistance.

At its most ardent, it wants to give itself entirely to what it discovers, as when her poem 'Over 2000 Illustrations and a Complete Concordance' concludes by asking 'Why couldn't we have . . . looked and looked our infant sight away'?

This is to say that Bishop's famous gift for observation is more than a habit of simply watching; it represents rather a certain self-conquest, the surmounting of a definite temperamental wariness. She is more naturally fastidious than rhapsodic. If she is well enough disposed towards the phenomena, she is still not exultant. Her detachment is chronic, and yet the combination of attentiveness and precision which she brings to bear upon things is so intense that the detachment almost evaporates. What Bishop does is to scrutinize and interrogate things as they are before giving her assent to them. She does not immediately or necessarily glorify them, being more of a sympathetic adjudicator than a born cheer-leader, but neither does she refuse them their just measure of praise. Her sense of reality, to put it another way, is more earth-bound than angelic. (. . .)

Within recent American poetry, Bishop occupies a position analogous to that long occupied on the other side of the ocean by Philip Larkin. In an era of volubility, she seems to demonstrate that less is more. By her sense of proportion and awareness of tradition, she makes what is an entirely personal and contemporary style seem continuous with the canonical poetry of the past. She writes the kind of poem that makes us want to exclaim with admiration at its professional thoroughness, its technical and formal perfections, and yet at the same time she tempts us to regard technical and formal matters as something of a distraction, since the poem is so candidly *about* something, engaged with its own business of observing the world and discovering meaning.

—Seamus Heaney, *The Redress of Poetry* (New York: Farrar, Straus, and Giroux, 1995): pp. 171–174.

MARILYN MAY LOMBARDI ON BISHOP'S RELATION
TO WALLACE STEVENS

[Marilyn May Lombardi teaches at the University of North Carolina, Greensboro. She has edited a collection of essays on

Bishop entitled *Elizabeth Bishop: The Geography of Gender* (1993) and is the author of *The Body and the Song: Elizabeth Bishop's Poetics* (1995). According to Lombardi, "The Monument" responds to the self-consciousness and elitism that inform Wallace Stevens's conception of art by privileging an aesthetic of the unconscious, the communal, the historical.]

Bishop's youthful experiments with surrealism, in which she strove to subvert logical control, culminated in "The Monument." At least in part, the poem was written as an antidote to a central image employed by Stevens in "Old Woman and the Statue" and "Mr. Burnshaw and the Statue," two works from *Owl Clover* (published in 1936) that seemed to glorify the artist's rational mastery of his material. Writing to Marianne Moore, Bishop explains that she cannot help reading *Owl Clover* as Stevens's "defense of his own poetic position," and the ubiquitous statue as his "conception of art," a conception that struck her as moribund, "confessing the 'failure' of such ART . . . to reach the lives of the unhappiest people," the people most hard hit by the depression, the people whose ideas of health and happiness are shaped largely by the mail order catalog (5 December 1936, RM). Stevens's notion of art, like Yeats's Platonic tower, stands as the last outpost of genteel minds, a fortress besieged by craven women and the uncouth poor, who represent the forces of irrationality at work in the world. (. . .)

In a Key West notebook, Bishop uses the Freudian-laced terms of surrealism to argue that poetry should include traces of its unconscious origins and a hint of the uncontrollable depths from which the writing has sprung: "What I tire of quickly in Wallace Stevens is the self-consciousness—poetry so aware lacks depth. Poetry should have more of the unconscious spots left in" (KW 289). A year after telling Moore of her misgivings about *Owl Clover*, Bishop started to form a clear image of her "monument," one that would employ the hallucinatory techniques of Max Ernst to expose the darkness and turmoil carefully excluded from Stevens's conception of art. (. . .)

We have in "The Monument" one of the first instances of what would become a common genre for Bishop—the poem that consciously reflects back on the processes of artistic creation. In the poem's final passage, we are told that the "monument" is the "beginning of a painting, a piece of sculpture, or poem" (*CP* 25), and, like any product of the imagination, it was engendered by an amorphous sea of associations. As the dialogue structure of "The Monument" suggests, the poet is trying to reconstruct the process by which associations give rise to a work of art, whether that artifact is a construct of wood or of words. (. . .)

The monument gives concrete shape not only to the idiosyncratic dreams of the poet but to the collective obsessions of a whole culture. It is a vast image out of the *spiritus mundi*, the universal reservoir of memories, eternally flowing and flown, which we will encounter again in "At the Fishhouses" (*CP* 66). There is, after all, something all-inclusive about the culture-laden monument. Its crowning fleur-de-lis is a relic of glory and conquest, a moldering sign of human history. Though the particular occasion commemorated by this cenotaph may have long ago died out of human memory, the desire to commemorate lives on and is embodied in the monument's sagging but surprisingly durable form. It seems to stand for the reconstructive spirit of art itself.

Still, the history that this pile of wood recounts, with its royal and ecclesiastical ornaments, is fundamentally elitist and, like the high modernism of Eliot or Stevens, removed from the lives of the unhappiest people. The two voices of the poem vacillate in their responses to the monument's modernist ambiguity, oscillating between interest and antipathy. The question for Bishop seems to be whether poetry can remain true to itself while touching the lives of a wider audience and whether that goal might be accomplished by showing that audience how flexible and accommodating art can be once it makes room for the arbitrary and the accidental. Reacting against Stevens's overly polished "statues," Bishop proposes a make-shift structure to which remnants of history have been "carelessly nailed" (*CP* 24). In a constant state of revision, growing, unfolding, changing, it is alive to possibility, always wanting "to cherish something." In the end, we as readers are enjoined to share in the collective enterprise by "decorating" the monument with our own impressions and contributing to the communal meaning of the *frottage*.

—Marilyn May Lombardi, *The Body and the Song: Elizabeth Bishop's Poetics* (Carbondale: Southern Illinois University Press, 1995): pp. 178–181.

[David Bromwich teaches at Yale University, where he is Housum Professor of English. His books include *Hazlitt: the Mind of the Critic* (1983), *Disowned By Memory: Wordsworth's Poetry of the 1790's* (1999), and *Skeptical Music* (2001), from which the following extract is drawn. Here Bromwich takes the monument as Bishop's figure for a poem as he examines the quality of self-assurance that runs through her work.]

Both words converge on a trait which all of Bishop's readers have felt in her poems: the presence of an irresistible self-trust. To her, art is a kind of home. She makes her accommodations with an assurance that is full of risk, and, for her as for Dickinson, the domestic tenor of some poems implies a good-natured defiance of the readers she does not want. The readers she cares for, on the other hand, are not so much confided in as asked to witness her self-recoveries, which have the quality of a shared premise. Her work is a conversation which never quite takes place but whose possibility always beckons. My point of departure in testing what this feels like in practice is an early poem, "The Monument." Bishop appears to have conceived it as an oblique eulogy for herself, and she frames it deferentially enough to suit a posthumous occasion. (. . .)

Irony, in one of its meanings, is a pretense of concern in a speaker, for the sake of revising a listener's whole structure of concerns; the pretense here is that Bishop's listener, in order to cherish the monument, need only hear it described just so. She patiently adjusts the description ("It is X. No. Like several X's . . .") to anticipate any complaint, as later in the poem she will give the listener a more official embodiment by composing speeches for him. All this self-qualification is a gravely enacted farce. When it is over we will find ourselves still staring at the monument and rehearsing what she has said about it, until we see that the object of the poem was to compel our attention without giving reasons.

In the course of the one-woman narration, with its imagined interruptions, we listeners are permitted exactly four objections to the monument. These may be summarized abstractly: I don't understand what this thing is trying to be; I've never seen anything hang together like this; It's just too makeshift to succeed; and, What are you trying to prove, anyway? In short, museum-boredom ("Big deal; take me somewhere else"), which the poet meets at first with a curatorial delicacy. But her final speech, which takes up almost a third of the poem, overcomes all defensiveness and simply expands the categorical authority of her earlier statement, "It is the monument." (. . .)

Earlier in the poem, still explaining the look of the monument itself, Bishop had composed a diagram of the viewer's relation to what he sees, which may also be read as a geometric proof of her own power over her readers.

> The monument is one-third set against
> a sea; two-thirds against a sky.
> The view is geared
> (that is, the view's perspective)
> so low there is no "far away,"
> and we are far away within the view.

I take the first five lines to mean that our eye is placed just above horizon level, so that the whole sky and sea appear as a flat vertical backdrop, without depth and therefore without any far or near. But in what sense can we be said to be "far away within the view"? It must be that the view looks out at us too, as through the wrong end of a telescope, from a perspective capable of absorbing everything: it takes us in as it pleases. Indeed, the monument can contain the world, by implication. That is the sense of the listener's disturbed question, "Are we in Asia Minor, / or in Mongolia?"—site of "Kubla Khan," where a kindred monument was decreed by imaginative fiat. So the poem says here, with the metaphor of perspective, what it says at the end by the rhetoric of conjecture: an active mind alone makes the world cohere, as "Wood holds together better / than sea or cloud or sand could by itself, / much better than real sea or sand or cloud." The flat declaration, "It chose that way to grow and not to move," only seems to announce a faith in the autonomy of art objects; Bishop returns us to the human bias of the thing, by her emphasis on those features of the monument which "give it away as having life, and wishing; / wanting to be a monument, to cherish something." Before it can be, it must want to be something. And we read it for whatever spirit it communicates; we cannot do more than watch. But we are accompanied by the prowling sun which also keeps watch—a casual sublimity, the reward of the poet's discovery of a shelter uniquely right for herself. It is an image to which Bishop will return in "The End of March," where the "lion sun . . . who perhaps had batted a kite out of the sky to play with," is mysteriously connected with the wire leading out from her dream-house "to something off behind the dunes."

—David Bromwich, *Skeptical Music* (Chicago: University of Chicago Press, 2001): pp. 117–120.

"Roosters"

"Roosters," which appeared in Bishop's first collection of verse, *North and South* (1946), is typically viewed as something of an anomaly in the context of her oeuvre, since the poem touches upon contemporary politics and Christian morality, topics Bishop often shied away from in the interest of avoiding the didacticism that characterized the "tract poetry," as she put it in an interview, she did not care for. The poem's sources are varied, ranging from a newspaper reproduction of one of Picasso's works, to aerial photos of the Nazi invasion of Finland and Norway at the start of World War II. Bishop's tercets consist of two-, three-, and four-stress lines—a pattern reminiscent of Richard Crashaw's "Wishes to his supposed Mistress," and the poem divides into three parts. The first describes the awakening of a small town by the "uncontrolled, traditional cries" of roosters, a movement that ends as the poem abruptly relocates the figure of the rooster, which comes to "mean forgiveness" in the context of a "small scene" drawn from "Old holy sculpture" concerning Peter's betrayal of Christ. The third and final movement of the poem returns to the scene of the slow dawn in the speaker's backyard, though now the "cocks are. . . almost inaudible," and ends by evoking a skepticism of any convenient epiphanic resolution of contraries. Like the sleepers, Peter, and the roosters—and the poems presents each with a pair of opposed faces or meanings—the sun is portrayed under the aspect of an either/or logic, "faithful as enemy, or friend."

The pocm opens with the pre-dawn crowing of "the first cock," and the responses, which Bishop figures as an echoing, of other neighboring roosters until "all over town begins to catch," as if their insistent cries were a burgeoning blaze. The darkness is "gun-metal blue," a phrase that appears in both of the first two stanzas and evokes the idea of military violence the poem elaborates. "Cries galore" continue to accumulate as Bishop elaborates a satiric portrait of masculine aggressiveness and militarism. The "green-gold medals" that image the roosters' showy feathers also evokes the pompousness and arrogance of military glory, while the "tin rooster" of the weathervane the poem associates with dictators or generals "marking out maps." That each of the roosters represents "an active/displacement in perspective" construes the military aggressors they stand for as narrow-minded, intolerant, attentive only to their own interests. Also built into the satire is a mocking portrayal of the failure to see through the rooster's gaudy show of authority. The "rustling wives" who submit to "lives/of being courted and despised" because of their ill-conceived admiration for the roosters are also satirized. Roosters and hens, aggression and submission, are implicated in a cyclic dynamic the speaker laments the inevitability and pointlessness of: after fighting, one rooster's "raging heroism" comes to nothing as it is "flung/on the gray ash-heap, lies in dung/with his dead wives," his "metallic feathers"—formerly likened to military decorations—undergoing a slow decay through oxidation.

Awakened prematurely, the speaker questions the roosters' "right ...to give/commands and tell us how to live," questions that go hand-in-hand with the poem's satirical critique of aggression. However, just as the poem presents a pair of distinct perspectives on the significance of the roosters, unsettling the judgments its satire calls for, so it unsettles an easy identification with the speaker as well, by locating her "here," in a place "where are/unwanted love, conceit and war." The roosters represent violence and arrogance, but the terms of the speaker's satire suggest they also stand as a reminder to "Get up!" or awaken from the state of complacent indifference in which the sleepers ignore not only "conceit and war," but also "love."

The instability of the role the roosters play in the poem's opening evolves into a full-fledged reversal of their emblematic significance in the middle section of the poem. Unlike poetry, Bishop's speaker somewhat enviously implies, "Old holy sculpture" can represent "past and future" together "in one small scene." The scene recuperates and transforms the rooster, as well as the imagery and ideas associated with it, even as the rooster stands within the scene as a figure of transformation, a "pivot" between Peter's denial of Christ and his eventual remorse. The rooster is here "our chanticleer," while his "vulgar beauty of iridescence" is refigured in the "tears" that cover his "sides and gem his spurs." Similarly, rather than "projecting" anything or "marking out maps," the roosters in the sculpture merely "waits," his "cries" and "screaming" become "cock-a-doodles" that "might bless." This moment of transfiguration is commemorated by "a bronze cock on a porphyry/pillar" that legitimatizes this non-aggressive version of the rooster even as it serves "to convince/all the assembly" that the rooster's cry is not only one of denial.

The last five stanzas turn back from the ecphrastic second movement of the poem to continue the account of the backyard dawn the roosters initially announced. The point of view shifts from the static and elevated realm of sculpture to register the gradual processes of nature from "underneath," as the "low light" of the sun gilds "the broccoli, leaf by leaf." The focus on militarism and aggression yields to a focus on Christian forgiveness, which in turn yields to a focus on nature, but Bishop is careful to preserve the disjunctive quality of the poem so as not to endorse any one perspective or frame a facile resolution of the rooster's contradictory symbolic meanings. Now almost "inaudible," the roosters have withdrawn along with their "senseless order," but the new order introduced by the sun is also unstable, ambiguous, as its faithfulness is likened to that of an "enemy, or friend."

CRITICAL VIEWS ON

"Roosters"

BISHOP COMMENTS ON THE POEM

[The following excerpts are drawn from a letter Bishop wrote to her friend and mentor Marianne Moore on October 17, 1940. She responds here to Moore's suggested revisions of "Roosters," defending the form and diction of the poem as it stands even as her intermittent self-deprecations speak to her respect for Moore's authority.]

What I'm about to say, I'm afraid, will sound like ELIZABETH KNOWS BEST. However, I *have* changed [the first words of each line of "Roosters"] to small initial letters! and I have made several other of your corrections and suggestions, and left out one of the stanzas . . . But I can't seem to bring myself to give up the set form, which I'm afraid you think fills the poem with redundancies, etc. I feel that the rather rattletrap rhythm is appropriate—maybe I can explain it.

I cherish my "water-closet" and the other sordidities because I want to emphasize the essential baseness of militarism. In the first part I was thinking of Key West, and also of those aerial views of dismal little towns in Finland and Norway, when the Germans took over, and their atmosphere of poverty. That's why, although I see what *you* mean, I want to keep "tin rooster" instead of "gold," and not use "fastidious beds." And for the same reason I want to keep as the title the rather contemptuous word ROOSTERS rather than the more classical THE COCK; and I want to repeat the "gun-metal." (I also had in mind the violent roosters Picasso did in connection with his *Guernica* picture.)

About the "glass-headed pins": I felt the roosters to be placed here and there (by their various crowings) like the pins that point out war projects on a map—maybe I haven't made it clear enough. And I wanted to keep "to see the end" in quotes because, although it may not be generally recognized, I have always felt that expression used of Peter in the Bible to be extremely poignant.

It has been so hard to decide what to do, and I know that esthetically you are quite right, but I can't bring myself to sacrifice what (I think) is a very important "violence" of tone—which I feel to be helped by what *you* must feel to be just a bad case of the *Threes* [EB wrote "Roosters" in triplet form]. (. . .)

I've kept this [foregoing] letter the last two days while I pondered some more over the poem, and now when I reread it, I think it sounds decidedly *cranky*. But you know I'm not and that you are the one who should be very cranky and cross with me for being so mulish. May I keep your poem? It is so interesting, what you have done—almost what Louise would call a "swing" version, I think. I'm about to go up to Pittsfield for the concert there and I'll be coming back sometime tomorrow. Could you be persuaded to the Klee show sometime in the week?—that is, if your cold is entirely cured. I'll send a copy of the poem as I *think* it is now—or is that adding insult to injury?. . .

—Elizabeth Bishop, One Art, ed. Robert Giroux (New York: Farrar, Straus and Giroux, 1994): pp. 96–97.

LOUISE BOGAN REVIEWS *NORTH AND SOUTH*

[Louise Bogan (1897–1970) was Poetry Editor of *The New Yorker* from 1931 until 1969 and a distinguished poet in her own right. *Blue Estuaries* (1968) collects her poetry from 1923 to 1968. For Bogan, *North and South* introduces a poet gifted with a natural style, a keen eye for detail, a subtle sense of humor, and a formal range and flexibility that allow her to explore "whatever catches her attention."]

It is a hopeful sign when judges unanimously and with enthusiasm make an award to a young, fresh book of verse instead of to an old, stale one. Last year, the three judges of the Houghton Mifflin Poetry Prize Fellowship did that in the case of Elizabeth Bishop's *North & South*, now published by Houghton Mifflin. Miss Bishop's poems, moreover, are not in the least showy. They strike no attitudes and have not an ounce of superfluous emotional weight, and they combine an unforced ironic humor with a naturalist's accuracy of observation, for Miss Bishop, although she frequently writes fantasy, is firmly in touch with the real world and takes a Thoreaulike interest in whatever catches her attention. She can write descriptions of New England and of Florida seascapes, of a mechanical toy, of boats and leaves in the Seine, of a city dawn, or of a mysterious pile of old boxes. And she has unmistakably her own point of view, in spite of her slight addiction to the poetic methods of Marianne Moore. Like Miss Moore, Miss Bishop, thoroughly canvassing all sides of a central idea, will make a poem out of one extended metaphor (as in "The Imaginary Iceberg"). Or she will bring into imaginative relation with one central theme a variety of subjects, making a poem out of a list of things or attributes related to a title (as in "Florida"). She often starts with a realistic subject, which, by the time she has unravelled all its concealed meaning, turns out to be the basis for a parable—the poem "Roosters," for example, contains all manner of references to war and warriors. Miss Bishop is a natural lyricist as well, but she does not use her lyrical side as often as she might. None of these thirty poems gives up its full meaning at once, so it is a pleasure to read them repeatedly. Miss Bishop has evidently put in eleven years on their composition; the first appeared in print in 1935. It is to be hoped that we shall get thirty more, equally varied, unexpected, and freshly designed, in rather less than another decade

—Louise Bogan, review of *North and South*, *The New Yorker* (October 5, 1946): pp. 113. Reprinted in *Elizabeth Bishop and Her Art*, ed. Lloyd Schwartz and Sybil Estess (Ann Arbor: University of Michigan Press, 1983): pp. 182–183.

WILLARD SPIEGELMAN ON HEROISM

[Willard Spiegelman has written *The Didactic Muse: Scenes of Instruction in Contemporary American Poetry* (1989) and *Wordsworth's Heroes* (1985) and teaches at Southern Methodist University. In the following extract Spiegelman compares Bishop to Wordsworth as he examines how her idea of heroism is exemplified in "Roosters."]

If anything, heroism and nature are antithetical. In Bishop's work, however, the "natural hero" occupies a privileged position which is unattainable by the super- or un-natural exploits of masculine achievement which the poetry constantly debunks. For Bishop, as for Stevens, "the man-hero is not the exceptional monster." This, in itself, is nothing new: ever since Wordsworth attempted to democratize the language and the subjects of poetry, his Romantic heirs have focused on ordinariness and on the self-conscious meditative habits which turn heroism inward. But Bishop goes beyond even Wordsworth's radical break with the past. Her hero replaces traditional ideas of bravery with a blend of domestic and imaginative strengths. The highest value in Bishop's work is a politely sceptical courage which neither makes outrageous demands on the world nor demurely submits to the world's own.

To understand Bishop's natural heroism, and her kinship with, yet movement beyond, Wordsworth, I wish to look at three types of poems, all tinged with her qualifying scepticism. First, there are those which trace the outline of heroic situations or devices and then negate or undercut them; second, those which internalize an encounter or conflict and, in the manner of a Romantic crisis lyric make the act of learning itself a heroic process, but which also dramatize the avoidance of apocalypse that Geoffrey Hartman has located at the heart of Wordsworth's genius; and finally those in which the *via negativa* of denial or avoidance implies Bishop's positive values, poems where a dialectical struggle between two contestants is resolved by an assertion of heroic worth. (. . .)

The clichés of masculine conquest are exploded in "Brazil, January, 1502," and in the first half of "Roosters." (. . .)

The bravado, false heroics, and metallic sheen of the cocks, for example, as well as the speaker's scorn and patronizing amusement, are replaced in the second half of "Roosters" by a new perspective and a softer voice. No longer mock warriors, the roosters become emblems of human sin and the promise of Christian forgiveness. Peter's denial of Christ at the cock's crowing is sculpted in stone as a tangible reminder of his weakness and his master's love. Even the little rooster is "seen carved on a dim column in the travertine." If you look hard enough, in other words, the fighting cock of the first part of the poem can be seen anew. Peter's tears and the cock's call are bound together, both in action and its symbolic representation:

"There is inescapable hope, the pivot;/ yes, and there Peter's tears/ run down our chanticleer's/ side and gem his spurs." As Peter was long ago forgiven, so we still learn that "'Deny deny deny' / is not all the roosters cry." Spurs encrusted with tears mark the transformation of militancy into humility. (. . .)

Bishop returns to her opening picture of daybreak, and the difference in her imagery alerts us to the distance between braggadocio and the roosters' subsequent Christian meekness. The opening was a military fanfare: (. . .)

The final view moves us to a slightly later stage of the dawn, gentler and tamed, as the roosters have literally ceased to crow, their threat having been figuratively replaced by the promise of forgiveness and natural harmony: (. . .)

Moving as it is, "Roosters" is not typical of Bishop's work. For one thing, the vocabulary of Christian belief appears only rarely in her poetry, and her imagination is more secular than religious (. . .)

For another, the studied symmetry, the juxtaposition of opposing views which augment one another, seems too easy.

—Willard Spiegelman, "Elizabeth Bishop's 'Natural Heroism,'" *Centennial Review* 22, no. 7 (Winter 1978): pp. 28–32.

VICTORIA HARRISON ON WAR POETRY

[Victoria Harrison teaches at the University of California, Santa Barbara and is the author of *Elizabeth Bishop's Poetics of Intimacy* (1993), from which the following extract is drawn. Harrison looks at how "Roosters" refuses the conventions of war poetry, particularly in the way it subtly implicates the sleepers in the world of aggression and conflict to which they are awakened.]

By 1940, when the war industry was gearing up in Key West, the actual war moved inward on her. Her poetic response was "Roosters," which relentlessly juxtaposes the dailiness of lovers in bed and the violence of war, undermining any myth of moral righteousness outside war. "Roosters" is skinned of the frames of pastoral harmony and dream. It opens by lurching from bed to battlefield: (. . .)

Real roosters crow here, but since these roosters very quickly take on human characteristics, this poem can, again, be seen within the tradition of animal fable. Yet these roosters are unreliable creatures, posing variously as barnyard animals, personifications, art in the form of weather vanes, and symbols within a Christian allegory of betrayal and redemption. Unsettling any comfortable interpretation, the poem's stanza form and rhyme insist on themselves—twelve *k* sounds, for instance, in the first fifteen lines—and relentless triplets and two-syllable rhymes.

As personifications, these roosters enact human behavior in its jarring extremes, (. . .)

The hens are passive, but for their masochistic activity of admiring the roosters who "command and terrorize" them. Admiration and a return in cruelty replace love; courting goes hand in hand with despising. When love becomes an irrelevant factor, power and authority are arranged in "a senseless order." One need go no farther than the barnyard to understand the human relations that make war possible, as Woolf outlined them in *Three Guineas*. But at the same time as she is personifying the roosters, Bishop implicates the human sleepers. They can scold the roosters for waking them, but they cannot extricate themselves from the world into which they are awoken:

> what right have you to give
> commands and tell us how to live,
>
> cry "Here!" and "Here!"
> and wake us here where are
> unwanted love, conceit and war?

"Unwanted love, conceit and war" are as intrinsic to the bed as to the battlefield; except there, enemies and friends are clearly, if artificially, demarcated for the soldier who must honor the distinctions. Though Mary Magdalen, the roosters' wives, the sleepers, and Christ are beyond the poem's direct censure, "Roosters" offers no clear means of separating roosters from humans or love and friends from conceit, war, and enemies.

Thus, the poem refuses to march forth with anger, horror, or disbelief at insensible war, as the great majority of war poetry does, choosing instead simple condescension toward fighting cocks. Bishop uses enjambment gracefully to offer the roosters a pedestal, only to shove them off,

> You, whom the Greeks elected
> to shoot at on a post,

further shriveling their supposed power with sarcasm:

> The crown of red
> set on your little head
> is charged with all your fighting blood.
>
> Yes, that excrescence
> makes a most virile presence,
> plus all that vulgar beauty of iridescence. (. . .)

Where the poem began in intrusive sound, it closes in relaxing sight. But the shift is only one of image and language; it signals neither closure nor transcendence of the poem's conflicts.

In its own refusal "to see the end" of any of the poem's concerns, the conclusion rejects a Christian righteousness with regard to war's depravity. The sun, finally, does not rise up and out of the poem. In its self-contradictory faithfulness, rather, it throws us back into the poem. To know whether one is friend or enemy seems an all-important task. National governments and their soldiers make these determinations confidently and rely on their authority. In its end and throughout, "Roosters" unsettles such a task, repeatedly setting the rooster up and dismissing as political and spiritual symbols that which we have conventionally rejected or relied upon. "To see the end" is, finally, to see how little closure there is, in the face of daily betrayals that cannot help but reflect the war's violation of supposedly sacrosanct values.

—Victoria Harrison, Elizabeth *Bishop's Poetics of Intimacy* (Cambridge: Cambridge University Press, 1993): pp. 89–91, 93.

JAMES LONGENBACH ON BISHOP'S POLITICS

[James Longenbach teaches at the University of Rochester and is the author of *Modern Poetry After Modernism* (1997), *Wallace Stevens: The Plain Sense of Things* (1991), and a collection of poetry entitled *Threshold* (1998). Here Longenbach discusses both "The Monument" and "Roosters" as he examines how Bishop's "social conscience" makes its way into her poems in spite of her overt distaste for "tract poetry."]

The problem for Bishop, early and late, was not her values as such but her discomfort—nurtured in the thirties—with the conventions of political poetry.

Bishop's values, especially her feminism, entered her poems in other ways. Characterizing her more recent reproachment with Bishop, Rich remarks that "poems examining intimate relationships" are replaced in Bishop's work by "poems examining relationships between people who are, for reasons of inequality, distanced: rich and poor, landowner and tenant, white woman and Black woman, invader and native." I would alter this insight to say that poems emphasizing social inequality do not take the place of poems emphasizing sexuality; rather, for Bishop, the consideration of gender and sexuality grew to be inseparable from the consideration of nationality or race. Missing in Bishop's poetry is almost the complete domain of what she thought of as political poetry; but from the beginning of her career, Bishop was "more interested in social problems" than, in retrospect, she would allow. (. . .)

Like several of the poems of *Owl's Clover*, "The Monument" oscillates between two voices, one sympathetic and the other hostile to the abstract and ambiguous monument. (. . .)

This defense of a "useless" artifact is a quintessential document of the 1930s—the decade in which the kind of modernist abstraction exemplified by Bishop's monument first came under attack. (. . .)

Yet Bishop's monument differs from other artistic icons (Keats's urn, Yeats's golden bird, or even Stevens's humble jar in Tennessee) in that it is made of wood, organic and decaying. Though it is more lasting than sea or sand, it does not offer refuge from reality. The monument is flawed, a little ridiculous, and undeniably human-made; its "crudest scroll-work says 'commemorate,'" suggesting that it is a monument to the potential grandeur of human folly and failure. Unlike "A Miracle for Breakfast" (which Bishop would later recall as a "'social conscious' poem" that was "written shortly after the time of souplines and men selling apples"), "The Monument" is not so obviously marked as a poem of the thirties; but it asks more rigorous questions about the relevance of art and imagination to (in the words of Bishop's letter about *Owl's Clover*) "the lives of the unhappiest people."

In contrast to "Then Came the Poor," "The Monument" doesn't show how the terms of gender may inflect those questions. But those terms became more consistently prominent in the poems Bishop began to write in Key West during the Second World War. In part, the reasons for this shift are cultural: the war emphasized the differences between the social roles occupied by men and women, and, at the same time, helped to obscure the prominent class differences of the Depression by offering an enemy common to all Americans. So while Bishop's "Roosters" is well-known as Bishop's war poem (. . .)

It is more precisely the poem's linkage of national and sexual aggression that marks it as a product of the Second World War. "Roosters" breaks into two halves, the first suggesting that the national aggression of war is essentially linked to masculinity: (. . .)

After the roosters have fought to the death and the body is flung on the ash-heap "with his dead wives," the poem considers a second way to understand a rooster's emblematic significance. Rather than invoking masculine aggression (and feminine passivity as its com-plement), their crowing now recalls St. Peter, who was reminded of his denial by a rooster: "'Deny deny deny' / is not all the roosters cry." But by introducing the New Testament significance of roosters in the second movement of the poem, Bishop isn't suggesting that the roosters' cries are not emblematic of masculine aggression; rather, she suggests that this association is far from essential or unchangeable. (. . .)

She asks her roosters, "what are you projecting?" but her poem makes us aware of what we project onto roosters: as emblems, the birds mean what we make them mean, and we are not doomed to war because of masculinity—or roosters—as such. At the end of the poem, when the sun rises "faithful as enemy, or friend," Bishop emphasizes the multiple significance of anything to which we grant emblematic meaning.

—James Longenbach, "Elizabeth Bishop's Social Conscience," *ELH* 62 (1995): pp. 468–469, 472–475.

DAVID BROMWICH ON BISHOP'S RELATION TO MARIANNE MOORE

[David Bromwich discusses "Roosters" in the context of Bishop's relationship with Marianne Moore and connects Bishop's subtle sense of identification with the roosters to the poem's late shift to a tone of humility.]

From beginning to end it covers the whole range from satire to prayer—from, if a parallel is wanted in Moore's work, the register of "To Be Liked by You Would Be a Calamity" to that of "In Distrust of Merits." I can point a moral by saying it is a poem of significantly characteristic private detestation, against all the acknowledged and audible legislators of the world whom the poet finds arrayed against herself, and whom she explicitly identifies as male. (. . .)

What can one learn about "Roosters" from the perspective opened up by its relationship to Moore? Like "Marriage," it is a protest against the people who most fiercely threaten the poet's imaginings, and who do so with the practical sanction of worldly authority. Those people are statesmen, businessmen, soldiers, husbands. The poet, who alone can displace them, is a woman not a wife. The grotesque feeling of the poem comes from the impression it makes of accurate hatred—an emotion only to be missed by those who have been tricked into insensibility by its rhymes. The pretense which the rhymes signal, of a satisfied striving for the minor effect, is, in fact, crueler in the end, as its ironies return upon the reader, than any comparable "undermining modesty" in Moore's early writing. Yet, for the reasons I have been tracing, this was an experiment which Bishop's reading of Moore led her to try. The strange thing about the partial retraction on which "Roosters" closes is that it touches just the note of humility that would become familiar above all in Moore's later work. And yet it does so before one can point to a movement as definitive in a single poem by Moore.

Humility itself may have a tactical value, as both of these poets recognized. Moore showed what that could mean in the way she chose to rewrite the last stanza or "Roosters." "The sun." Bishop had written,

> climbs in,
> following "to see the end."
> faithful as enemy, or friend.

Moore changed it to

> And climbing in to see the end,
> the faithful sin is here,
> as enemy, or friend.

That version is weaker than Bishop's as poetry for the same reason that it is clearer as morality (incorporating, as it does, the Peter-Christ parable, which Bishop left implicit at the close). Moore's revision, however, seems to me in line with the poem's argument in the last several stanzas. For by that point it has become a petition for forgiveness. It is the nature of roosters, Bishop concedes, to annoy, hector, tear, and fight for command. Though they break in to the poet's sleep and the dreaming life that comes with sleep, their denials are not unlike hers; as, for that matter, their "active displacements in perspective" are not unlike hers. (. . .)

As for Bishop's reasons for seeking forgiveness, they will remain obscure only so long as we look at her as a citizen and not a poet. Like the creatures she denounces, she is a reshaper of things in the world, and others will live with what she makes. There is one kind of poetry in an inventive reading of maps, another kind in the over-running of actual places on a map of conquest. Either way, the aim is to make a senseless order prevail. So Bishop's allusion to "marking out maps like Rand McNally's" is not the innocent detail it seems. It is carefully placed in this poem, by an author for whom "The Map" would become a kind of signature. Her sense, in allying herself with the roosters, of a complicity in all that she hates, may suggest that the withdrawal from satire here allowed Bishop to escape from a graver turning against herself.

—David Bromwich, *Skeptical Music* (Chicago: University of Chicago Press, 2001): pp. 109, 113–114.

"At the Fishhouses"

"At the Fishhouses" appeared in Bishop's second collection, *A Cold Spring* (1955), and exemplifies her characteristic tendency to legitimatize a privileged moment of understanding by representing it as the natural result of an exercise in observation. Before offering up the revelation that "our knowledge is historical, flowing and flown," the speaker first pays tribute to the artistry of nature through meticulous descriptions of land and sea that thematize notions of flux, repetition, and erosion. Like the "heavy surface of the sea,/swelling as if considering spilling over," the poem charts a gradual, wary progress toward an epiphany in which observation "spill[s] over" into a highly qualified vision—not of what knowledge is, but of something "like what we imagine [it] to be."

Like "Cape Breton," which follows "At the Fishhouses" in *A Cold Spring*, the poem returns to Bishop's Nova Scotia childhood for its setting. The poem's first sentence introduces a Wordsworthian solitary reminiscent of the leechgatherer in "Resolution and Independence" and the aged mendicant of "The Old Cumberland Beggar": "Although it is a cold evening," an old fisherman, who seems almost to blend into the scene he inhabits, sits working on his net. He is immersed in his work as he is immersed in the scene, circumstances that link him to the seal—like the speaker a "believer in total immersion"—that appears later in the poem. The slow paced, densely detailed description of the sights, sounds, and smells of the waterfront attests to the speaker's belief in immersion even as it invites the reader to share in that belief.

The emphatic fidelity to the setting evoked in the opening stanza foregrounds the speaker's respect for the complex and mutable aesthetic of nature—a respect made explicit in the accounts of the fisherman's "polished" shuttle, the "emerald moss" of the buildings, and the "beautiful" scales of the herrings that are described as "sequins" adorning the fisherman's vest and thumb. The unassuming character of the speaker's rhetoric in the initial stanza works a kind of self-effacement that implicitly reinforces the sublimity of the scene. The imagery of the stanza is concerned largely with registering the effects of the waning light, though this does not translate into a concern with color. "All is silver" on land and sea, and the speaker attends to variations in the intensity and character of the light to nuance her observations—translucence, opacity, iridescence, brightness. Where color does emerge through the silver glow of the scene, it is momentary, fugitive, indistinct: the "dark purple brown" of the net is "almost invisible," the "black old knife" is "worn" with use, the handles of the capstan are "bleached" from the weather. The liminal quality that inheres in both the scene's particulars and its general composition speaks to an idea of flux that recurs in the description of "knowledge" with which the poem concludes. Knowledge, like the waterfront scene the speaker elaborates, is conditioned by time and can only be captured momentarily and at a remove.

The speaker gives the old man a cigarette, a small act of charity that reinforces his resemblance to Wordsworth's Cumberland beggar, who depends in a similar way on the kindness of passersby for provisions. Bishop's fisherman is absorbed into the decadent aesthetic of nature—an aesthetic to which he contributes by scraping the scales "from unnumbered fish" until, like the wheelbarrows layered with an iridescent coat, his vest is decorated with "sequins." The relationship between the speaker and the fisherman evokes the idea of a communion with nature, but only to bring the essential detachment of the speaker from the natural world into even sharper relief. Their "talk"—of "the decline in population" and of "codfish and herring/while he waits for a herring boat to come in"—is insubstantial, polite, their exchange short-lived, their friendship an echo of a friendship that no longer exists: "He was a friend of my grandfather." Too, the dignity of the occasion is undercut to some extent by the slight suggestion of whimsical humor in the fisherman's acceptance of a "Lucky Strike." The speaker's relationship to the old man, like her relationship to the seal that appears later in the poem, is coded as an experiment in sympathy with nature, but in spite of these brief moments of connection, nature remains harsh and alienating, a realm in which the air "makes one's nose run and one's eyes water," and the temperature of the water ensures that "your bones would begin to ache and your hand would burn."

The transitional second stanza of the poem marks a shift of focus from land to sea as the beholder's gaze pauses for a moment at "the water's edge." The stanza functions as a sort of compass rose, and its language, with its repeated emphasis on direction—the "long ramp" that descends "into the water," the tree trunks "laid horizontally/ across" the stones—reflects a concern with reorientation. The speaker's gaze moves "down and down" from the old man and the "almost invisible" particulars of his environment to the sea and its impenetrable depths.

The final stanza of the poem begins with the same impulse to enumerate and describe that informs the depiction of the fishhouses in the first stanza, but the sea, "cold, dark, deep and absolutely clear," resists this treatment, and the speaker's observations trail off into a recognition of the harsh elementality of the sea and end in ellipsis. The sea's impenetrability prompts the speaker to alter her approach, and she turns her attention to her curious sense of relationship with a seal she has seen evening after evening. The seal, anthropomorphized in its curiosity, interest in music, and sense of judgment, is the figure of the sea just as the old fisherman is the figure of the waterfront. The speaker's relationship with the seal functions as a context for self-mockery, as the speaker admits her unreadiness to come to terms with the sea and its sublime inscrutability by imagining a communion with an animal founded on a mutual interest in music and a shared belief in "total immersion." The speaker sings "A Mighty Fortress is Our God," and the idea of a reassuring permanence implicit in the title signals her continuing concern with the difficulty of confronting the flux of nature. Even the seal seems to catch on to this underlying tension, as his apparently quizzical regard and "shrug/as if it were against his better judgment" seem to suggest. As if parodying in advance the speaker's effort to describe the sea, he emerges "almost in the same spot," just as the speaker emerges from her digression nearly at the point she left it, reiterating her initial description but then abandoning it with an ellipsis: "Cold, dark, deep and absolutely clear,/the clear gray icy water. . . ." The poem's shift from a descriptive anecdotal register to one of speculation and meditation occurs when the speaker discovers a rhetoric adapted to her awed ocean-gazing. Instead of the objective, exhaustively various account she provides of the waterfront—and twice fails to provide of the sea—she perceives the sea in its repetitive sameness and uses a more figurative, qualified idiom to make assertions: the water "seems" to be suspended; wrist and bones "would" ache "if" dipped in the water. The speaker succeeds in immersing herself in the previously unbearable water, but at a remove revealed through the second-person point of view and conditional narration.

In the poem's final sentence the water—"dark, salt, clear, moving, utterly free"—becomes an analogue for knowledge, though this connection is doubly qualified: the water is only similar to what we "imagine knowledge to be." Knowledge, like the speaker's imagined baptism, is available only at a remove, mediated by an epistemological framework. The sentence replays the tendencies for personification and anthropomorphism evident in the speaker's discovery of human (and humanized) representatives of both land and sea earlier in the poem, imagining the "world" with a "cold hard mouth" and "rocky breasts." Knowledge, like the decaying waterfront, is subject to the flux of nature, and the speaker represents it in the poem's final line under the aspect of the temporal: "our knowledge is historical, flowing and flown."

CRITICAL VIEWS ON

"At the Fishhouses"

DAVID KALSTONE ON THE PASTORAL TRADITION

[The late David Kalstone taught at Rutgers University until his
death in 1986. His publications include *Sidney's Poetry* (1965),
his classic *Five Temperments* (1977), and *Becoming a Poet*
(1989). In the extract that follows Kalstone places "At the
Fishhouses" in the context of the pastoral tradition, analyzing
the way the dense description of the opening stanzas sets up
the discovery with which the poem concludes.]

"In the Village" was intimately related to the travel poems among
which it was set—the darker side of their serene need to reclaim "the
elements speaking: earth, air, fire, water." That particular necessity
lies behind one of Miss Bishop's finest poems, "At the Fishhouses,"
set, as the story was, in Nova Scotia. It opens with an intense,
lengthy description: (. . .)

Like one of Stevens' pastorals, Miss Bishop's is a scene almost
without a spectator, the speaker comically unwelcome in an air
which smacks of another element and which makes her eyes water
and her nose run. She slowly exposes the scene, present tense, with
a tempered willingness to let it speak for itself in a kind of declarative simplicity. Things *are*; things *have*. The lone fisherman, a
Wordsworthian solitary, is faded into the scene, his net "almost
invisible," his shuttle "worn and polished," his "black old knife"
with a blade "almost worn away." The dense opening description—
deliberately slow, fifty lines of the poem—is in all details of sight
and sense and sound intended to subject us to the scene, to draw us
deeply into it. "The five fishhouses have steeply peaked roofs / and
narrow, cleated gangplanks slant up . . .": even the insistent conso-
nants and the doubling of adjectives force those words apart and
force us to dwell on them, as if to carve out some certainty of vision.
We are to become what the speaker claims for herself later in the
poem: "a believer in total immersion." From that immersion a pattern gathers, unhurried but there: present, for example, in the odd

half-rhyme of *codfish* and *polished* or in the unassuming repetition of *iridescent*. The wheelbarrows are "plastered / with creamy iridescent coats of mail, / with small iridescent flies crawling on them." The crudeness and delicacy of these details are made to appear strokes of the same master, of the landscape's age-old subjection to the sea, to the caking, the plastering, the lining, the silvering-over which turns everything to iridescence or to sequins at the same time as it rusts them, wears away, erodes.

In its fidelity to setting—to what is both jagged and strangely jewelled—the poem accumulates the sense of an artistry beyond the human, one that stretches over time, chiseling and decorating with its strange erosions. The human enterprise depends upon and is dwarfed by the sea, just as the fish-house ramps lead out of and back into the water: (. . .)

The poet returns knowledge to concreteness, as if breaking it down into its elements ("dark, salt, clear . . ."). The speaker herself seems drawn into the elements: at first jokingly in the fishy air which makes the nose run, the eyes water; then in the burning if one dips one's hand, as if water were a transmutation of fire that feeds on stones. (. . .)

With a final fluency she leaves her declarative descriptions behind and captures a rhythm at once mysterious and acknowledging limitations: "flowing and drawn . . . flowing and flown." Her earlier submission to the scene has prepared the way for a momentary freedom in nature; the poem realizes one of Stevens' promises, "refreshes life so that we share / For a moment the first idea." From its Theocritean beginnings as a variety of communal song and performance (such was the fiction the poem maintained), pastoral becomes an effort at limning out private discoveries. Miss Bishop's poem is one example of how completely landscape has taken over the substance of such poems and how it can assume an individualizing force. The poet, now more spectator than singer, recognizing dependencies, measures his mind against and by means of natural detail.

—David Kalstone, "Conjuring With Nature," *Twentieth-Century Literature in Retrospect*, ed. Reuben Brower (Cambridge: Harvard University Press, 1971): pp. 264–268.

[Elizabeth Spires is the author of several acclaimed collections of poetry, including *Globe* (1981), *Annonciade* (1989), and *Worldling* (1995). In the following extract Spires interprets the poem as a meditation on the limits of knowledge in which Bishop "insists that what little we know to be true keeps changing."]

"At the Fishhouses" by Elizabeth Bishop is a meditation on empirical knowledge vs. absolute truth, the human problem of 'netting' or knowing anything with any degree of certainty in a physically ever-changing world. As the poem opens, Bishop details a darkening Nova Scotian landscape in literal and metaphorical decline. Early on, the poet introduces the means by which the scene is to be mediated, the five senses represented by the five fishhouses, the senses mediating between the mind ("storerooms in the gables") and the external world. All five senses come strongly into play as the poem progresses. Land and water are seen as distinctly opposed entities with the poem's stanzaic structure reinforcing this opposition. The descriptive focus of the first stanza centers on land whose silver surfaces at dusk are of "an apparent translucence." In contrast, the sea is opaque and apparently conscious, described as "swelling slowly as if considering spilling over," its silver surface hiding a quite different kind of knowledge, one not necessarily apprehended by the senses. And yet, the word "apparent" qualifies the land's seeming translucence, hinting at illusion or disguise and suggesting limits on what can be known or apprehended even as we stand on solid ground.

The emphasis then in the dense descriptive lines of the first stanza is on the *appearance* of things. The old man, both Time personified and in time himself, links the invisible past of the poet's dead grandfather with the immediate present: (. . .)

The repetitive physical action described parallels the eroding action of time itself and places an implicit value on surface appearance: the fish scales, likened to sequins, are, importantly, "the principal beauty," the flies crawling on the fish tubs "iridescent." The old man's knife is talismanic, an earlier incarnation, we can guess, of Crusoe's knife in "Crusoe in England." (. . .)

The sea, as a representation of absolute knowledge, of knowledge out of time, is an "element bearable to no mortal," in stark opposition to the half-truths and "apparent" perceptions of ordinary human existence. The gravity of the statement is counter-balanced by the seemingly playful scene with the seal. The seal's presence is crucial. Without it, the sea would be utterly inhuman and non-relational. The creature is presented as a skeptical, yet kindred intelligence, like the poet, "a believer in total immersion." The seal's bemused and curious reaction to the singing of "A Mighty Fortress Is Our God" raises the question as to the spirit in which the speaker sings the hymn. Seriously? Playfully? Presumably the latter, given the tone of the scene.

The haunting echo-effect of repeating the line "Cold dark deep and absolutely clear" moves the poem toward a powerful and sweeping conclusion. Behind the speaker and seal, temporally as well as spatially, "a million Christmas trees stand waiting for Christmas." The Christmas trees seem both hopeful and wistful projections, signifying perhaps the poet's yearning for the lost innocence of an earlier time. The value of repeated sensory experience is emphasized over the nostalgic or sentimental with the line, "I have seen it over and over," as if the senses were a means to at least a partial apprehension of a higher order of knowledge. The poet's desire for absolute knowledge, some contact with omniscience, through secular or poetic epiphany takes the form of an invitation to the reader to participate in a painful baptism: (. . .)

The utter physicality of the action is a comment on the limitations of the corporeal state as well as being a metaphoric statement: the body a metaphor for the spirit or soul, and one's ability to suffer or accept physical pain a metaphor for the soul's growth.

—Elizabeth Spires, "Questions of Knowledge," *Field* 31 (Fall 1984): pp. 20–22.

[Robert Dale Parker teaches at the University of Illinois at Urbana-Champaign and is the author of *Faulkner and the Novelistic Imagination* (1985) and *The Unbeliever* (1988), from which the following extract is drawn. Parker discusses the significance of the sea in the poem with specific regard to the strategies of delay and evasion that temper the poem's modulations from description into meditation.]

The unchanging world of the fish, finally, intrigues Bishop more: But she cannot turn to it easily. She spends half the poem working up to it by describing the land, then the fisherman, then, in a conspicuously transitional stanza, actually describing the ramp that descends from land to sea, as if she needs to find some feature in the physical landscape to draw her into the water, like a timid bather stepping in slowly. Then at last, and with tones of self-conscious profundity, she dives in: (. . .)

She introduces the water in an atmosphere of all-encompassing yet unspecifiable mystery. Its depth suggests an ultimacy, almost a ublquity; yet it is also distantly cold, too dark and clear to see. She so romanticizes, on the one hand, the ocean's grandiose allure and, on the other hand, its ominous invisibility that the combination of almost opposed extremes implies that ordinary ocean has little to do with what so attracts and intimidates her. Instead she puzzles over the role that ordinary ocean can somehow figure in her own partly private and partly representative array of fears and wishes.

The impulses to such figurings are vague but threatful, and hence not easy to own up to. Every time Bishop gets a start at them, she soon backs away. If the element she ruminates over is "bearable to no mortal," then what draws her to it? Hence the glibly cliché evasion, "to no mortal," lets her rationalize a further evasion. She slides into an ellipsis and changes the subject to animal—that is, to unambiguously mortal—comic relief, nervously relaxing with a little satire of her immersion in place and her preoccupation with water. Then she can move on. Moving on, therefore, means moving back to the words she left off with, the words before her ellipsis that were supposed to introduce her direct turn to the water, and that she left when she got fearful and distracted. But instead of returning to those words, she slides into yet another ellipsis, turning "Back, behind us" to the land of trees.

All this looping back adds up to a startling hesitation, as if both the length of her reluctance and the piling up of her repetitions measure the force of what she hesitates before. They evoke the sea's awesome breadth and uniformity; she can go back to it forever and always it will be "the same":

> I have seen it over and over, the same sea, the same,
> slightly, indifferently swinging above the stones,
> icily free above the stones,
> above the stones and then the world.

The land changes, the sea stays the same. Both evoke her past, one a fading past that soon she will recover only through memory, never through immediate sensation, and the other a past she can always recover. Strangely, because the sea's past never varies, it is somehow almost cosmically more capacious, and therefore less tangible than the past that escapes ubiquity to lodge in memory. That cosmic suggestiveness exacts from Bishop an awed humility, in which her repeated words and phrases ("the same," "above the stones") build an incantatory sound that culminates in the closing lines: (. . .)

The public knowledge celebrated in the final line is historical, received, in contrast to the asserted, original knowledge of "The Map," in which the printer's excitement reveals emotion that "exceeds its cause," tempting Bishop to think that the "countries pick their colors." The wished-for open sesame of imagination in early poems like "The Map" and "The Man-Moth" thus gives way to a resigned-to satisfaction at natural specificity in the poems of Bishop's mid-career. In "At the Fishhouses," the final, cadenced hush before "it," before the ocean, betrays how desperately in the first part of the poem Bishop strives to keep the evanescent place from slipping away before she can trap it in poetic capture.

—Robert Dale Parker, *The Unbeliever: The Poetry of Elizabeth Bishop* (Urbana: University of Illinois Press, 1988): pp. 80–82.

BONNIE COSTELLO ON NOTIONS OF FLUX IN THE POEM

[In the following extract from *Elizabeth Bishop: Questions of Mastery* (1991), Bonnie Costello examines the way "At the Fishhouses" renovates the model of the Romantic crisis lyric as it culminates in an acceptance of transience and uncertainty.]

Repeatedly her eye is led from images of a disintegrating order or hierarchy (often vertically defined) to images of transience. That transience forms an attractive array of details; but the eye gravitates toward an obscure center in the landscape which the poet associates with profundities and mysteries of origin and destiny. Instead of providing a resting place, these dark centers rebuff the imagination. The poet returns to surface and to flux as the only reality in which the consciousness can act. Often Bishop relates this return to the emergence of a figure in the foreground—an animal or person— which becomes associated with ineffable, momentary coalescence of being rather than with an articulate order or wisdom. This structure parallels but revises the greater Romantic lyric, with its hierarchical movement from description to meditation, its pattern of crisis and resolution or fall and redemption. Bishop's structure of observation and reflection turns away from transcendent idealism toward the acceptance of change as absolute. "At the Fishhouses" defines this structure of meditation most explicitly.

   In "At the Fishhouses" Bishop explores the atmosphere of decline in an eschatological vision. She follows her usual pattern of loose description which builds up only gradually to thematic focus. Again we find the characteristic movement: horizontal images of transience and mutability dominating over vertical images of permanence and stasis lead to an obscure center of meaning, from which the beholder is excluded; the attention returns to the foreground and then moves off to an emblematic image of mutability. (. . .)

   As the poem turns, at the end, to philosophical reflection, it remains tied to images, though they have become more explicitly figurative. (. . .)

The poem seemed to be moving toward eschatological questions, but swerves to take up epistemological ones instead, asking not what fate is, or what God is, but what knowledge is. Even the definition of knowledge is figurative and speculative, a metaphor within metaphor, as Bishop wrote in her notebook about our idea of God. Here, we "imagine" knowledge to be "like" the burning brine. This is hardly the certain rhetoric of epiphany. Our knowledge of knowledge, like our knowledge of everything else, remains mediated. Yet "knowledge" here (not reason but understanding) resembles existence itself. Bishop's definition of knowledge indeed becomes a definition of transient life, not a defense against it. Against the "small, old" fishhouses and even the mighty fortress of religion, Bishop provides us with an image of mother earth, as an unprotective source and destiny. The figurative language here, like the "ancient chill" in "Cape Breton," makes no metaphysical claims; this is the freedom of, not from, necessity, the freedom of flux from the storehouses in which we attempt to master it.

The fragmented female anthropomorphism of the "cold hard mouth" and "rocky breasts" denies the gendered ascendancy of Mind as source over Nature. Bishop subordinates "knowledge" to nature, making it subject to flux and perhaps identical with it. This unnurturing image nevertheless resists the obsession with apocalyptic ending that informs the poem elsewhere. If knowledge and life are "flowing, and flown," they are also "derived . . . forever" from these unnurturing breasts, "drawn" from this unspeaking mouth. Bishop's conclusion is anti-Romantic, antimetaphysical. What is deep is not murky but moving and clear. What resolution and independence the poem offers hinge upon this consciousness.

—Bonnie Costello, Elizabeth Bishop: Questions of Mastery
(Cambridge: Harvard University Press, 1991): pp. 109, 115–116

ANNE COLWELL ON THE THEME OF MEDIATION

[Anne Colwell is the author of *Inscrutable Houses* (1997), from which the following extract is drawn. Colwell explores the way notions of connection are problematized in "At the Fishhouses" by Bishop's commitment to reckoning the extent to which knowledge and experience are mediated.]

In "At the Fishhouses," one of the most exciting poems in *A Cold Spring* or anywhere, Bishop explores the rich ambivalence arising from the conflict between knowledge and change, connection and loss, history and eternity, life and death. Nowhere in the poem do these tensions collapse into chaos or even into order, into resolution. Instead, Bishop draws on the tensions, juxtaposes opposites within the same line, or thought, or word in order to embody in the poem's structure the evasive and elusive quality of knowledge that she finds in the world. Bishop moves from the apparently known to the unknowable, from the land to the sea, from powerful description to the realm where language falls silent, from connection to immersion. (. . .)

Bishop goes on to describe vividly the details of the land, all touched and changed by the sea but still knowable, still part of the land, the human milieu: (. . .)

The wheelbarrows lined with herring scales and the flies that live off of these scales connect the human-made objects to the natural world of the land. The absolute vividness of this description, Bishop's ability to re-create the physicality of the objects in the landscape, provides a way for the reader and the speaker to know the world, to connect momentarily with each other and with the scene.

This connection is amplified in the lines that follow by the connection the speaker makes between the old fisherman and herself: (. . .)

As in the opening lines of the poem, the old man seems both connected with and separate from the landscape that surrounds him. He seems a fixture; he has known the poet's grandfather. He, like everything human in this scene, is covered with the silvery herring scales. Like the speaker, the fisherman negotiates with the landscape he inhabits, by acting, waiting, attempting to find a living in the sea. Both speaker and fisherman are "netting," looking for sustenance from the sea, forging a connection. But for both, this connection is terribly ambivalent. In this stanza, the fisherman interacts with the world around him by scraping off "the principal beauty" of "unnumbered fish." This action parallels the violence and conflict implicit in the relationship between the seer and the contingent world in "A Cold Spring." Similar ambivalence and conflict occur in the relationship between the fisherman and the speaker, as the list of conversational topics demonstrates—all topics of common small talk but tinged with the threat of dissolution, of the failing of the community and the trade, all flatly delivered. (. . .)

In the last lines of the poem, Bishop switches to the second person and the reader is literally immersed in the poem; the moment of baptism, of connection, broadens to include the speaker's connection with the sea, the speaker's connection with the reader, and the reader's connection with the sea: (. . .)

The connection with the sea involves physically touching the icy water; this experience is knowledge, but the sea itself is not knowledge, but instead, and more importantly, "It is like what we imagine knowledge to be." Paradoxically, the connection that promised to draw the speaker and the reader out of themselves, perhaps to their own annihilation, actually forces both speaker and reader back into themselves and connects them to their own imaginations. This connection is not only paradoxical but frighteningly ambiguous. "At the Fishhouses" suggests that knowledge and connection may actually be mutually exclusive, that we cannot know what we experience because of our subjective walls, because of our flawed human senses, our tendency to imagine our own bodies everywhere. Thus, the sea Bishop finally put her hand in becomes a woman, has a "cold hard mouth" and "rocky breasts." She finally connects with the sea by taking it into herself, connects with the reader by taking him or her to the sea.

—Anne Colwell, *Inscrutable Houses: Metaphors of the Body in the Poems of Elizabeth Bishop* (Tuscaloosa: University of Alabama Press, 1997): pp. 115, 117–118, 121–122.

CRITICAL ANALYSIS OF

"Crusoe in England"

"Crusoe in England" evolved from Bishop's interest in re-seeing the experience of Defoe's famous Solitary with the Christian moralizing "left out," as she expressed it in an interview with George Starbuck. Too, it draws on the poet's abiding fascination with travel and geography, and a particular curiosity about "making things do—of using things in unthought of ways because of necessity"—a condition for which Crusoe's insular existence provides an ideal context to explore. A dramatic monologue, the poem was collected in Bishop's last published volume, *Geography III* (1976). Its exploration of the relation between imagination and survival repeatedly raises the issue of memory: a lonely, self-pitying, and nostalgic minor celebrity in England, Crusoe remembers the loneliness, self-pity, and nostalgia of his days on a more remote island.

News of the eruption of a "new volcano" and the discovery of an island prompt Crusoe's speech about his own volcanic island. "None of the books has ever got it right," he laments, a remark that situates the poem as a corrective to faulty official reports. The first stanza introduces a concern with documentation and language that recurs throughout the poem as Crusoe juxtaposes his "reading" in "papers and books" with his attempts to name and register what he observed and experienced. These attempts are represented as problematic in themselves. "The books/I'd read were full of blanks," he notes resignedly, and he forgets part of a Wordsworth poem that neither Defoe's Crusoe nor Defoe himself could have read. That he christens one of the volcanoes "*Mont d'Espoir* or *Mount Despair*" points up the arbitrariness of language, and later in the poem he recalls "nightmares" of "registering" the flora, fauna, and geography of "infinities of islands." The world-weariness audible in Crusoe's casual idiom seems to derive at least in part from a resigned awareness of the inadequacy of language.

The color, variety, and unique character of the island's life and geography are undercut by Crusoe's ambivalence about his island sojourn, an ambivalence that emerges in his understated, ironic rhetoric. "Well, I had fifty-two/miserable, small volcanoes I could climb/with a few slithery strides –/volcanoes dead as ash-heaps," he begins the second stanza, and much of what he observes is described in a similarly casual tone. Part of the effect of the speaker's resigned style is to underline his sense of estrangement from his surroundings, an estrangement also apparent in the fears that result from the disorientation the size of the volcanoes occasions: "if I had become a giant,/I couldn't bear to think what size/the goats and turtles were. . . ." Old standards of scale and proportion prove useless. Bishop's characteristic interest in perspective is evident here, as is her tendency to link meticulous observation and empiricism to the surreal: the more Crusoe perceives, the more unfamiliar reality becomes.

Before moving on to recount the life of the island and to describe his emotional responses to his situation, Crusoe provides an account of the climate and seas surrounding him in the third stanza of the poem. Just as the volcanoes are "miserable" and "small," so the island seems to him a "cloud-dump," the "overcast" sky inhabited by "left-over clouds" that hang above the hissing craters. The landscape continues to be depicted in all its exotic detail even as it is implicitly judged to be somehow inadequate, second-hand. The stanza also continues to rely on the figure of personification: the volcanoes, already portrayed with "their heads blown off," are represented with "parched throats," and the waterspouts advance and retreat with "their heads in cloud, their feet in moving patches/of scuffed-up white." The impulse to familiarize the environment through personification also comes through in his comparison of the turtles and waterspouts to "teakettles" and "chimneys"—which share in a notion of domestic familiarity he seems to yearn for. That the waterspouts are "Beautiful, yes, but not much company" makes the estrangement he associates with the experience of solitude explicit. Crusoe's loneliness causes him to indulge in a habit of self-pity and to question whether or not his shipwreck was decreed by fate or was something he chose. He asks, rhetorically, "What's wrong with self-pity anyway," and goes on to explain how he came to sanction feeling sorry for himself. He uses pity as a way of coming to terms with the otherness of his environment, whimsically stipulating that "Pity should begin at home," so that "the more/pity" he experiences, the more he feels "at home." It is his deep-seated longing for home that inspires his creation of the "home-made flute" he plays after drinking the "home-brew" he cautiously makes from the only berries he is able to find on the island. Amid the unique but limited resources of the island, which "had one kind of everything," Crusoe consoles himself by developing and cherishing several "island industries"—a moment in the poem that harkens back to Bishop's initial interest in exploring the connection between imagination and survival. But Bishop's Crusoe, unlike Defoe's, cannot rely on religion to help make sense of his situation. Instead he evolves "a miserable philosophy," impoverished by his lack of learning and telling forgetfulness: ironically, it is the world "solitude," so obviously relevant to Crusoe's situation, that he cannot recall from Wordsworth's "I Wandered Lonely as a Cloud."

Crusoe has "time enough to play with names," but the island world remains unsettlingly unfamiliar to him, even in the tiresome repetitiveness of its sights, sounds, and smells, and in spite of his attempts to accommodate its strangeness through invention and industry. This island proves no Edenic paradise, and the poem is thoroughly anti-pastoral: the cacaphonic noises of goats and gulls Crusoe "still can't shake" from his ears, and the uniform whiteness prompts him to dye a goat "bright red." This experiment can be seen as a cruel attempt to displace his own sense of alienation, or to master it by further defamiliarizing an environment that already seems unreal to him, as his yearning for "real shade" explicitly suggests.

The contrasting pair of names Crusoe assigns one of the volcanoes reflect the poem's polarized movement between hope of finding meaning in experience and despair at remembering such extremes of loneliness and estrangement. It is in keeping with this pattern that his account of his nightmares of endless islands directly precedes an account of Friday's arrival: "Just when I though I couldn't stand it/another minute longer, Friday came." Crusoe reiterates his intention of setting the record straight, as though the integrity of his relationship with Friday is something he is especially interested in protecting. Friday's arrival in the poem marks a change of rhetorical register, as Crusoe shifts from an elaborately figurative diction to an pointedly simple style: "Friday was nice./Friday was nice, and we were friends." The simplicity of the language reflects the depth and complexity of Crusoe's feelings for Friday by stressing his own inability to articulate them fully.

The poem's final movement concerns Crusoe's dissatisfaction with life back in England, "another island" on which he feels isolated, "bored" as he drinks his "real tea" amid "uninteresting lumber." Meaning, for Crusoe, seems only to exist in the past: just as he once yearned for the familiarities of life in England, so at the end of the poem he yearns for the restoration of the numinous quality that his knife, flute, shoes, and trousers possessed when they were essential to survival. But the "living soul" of his knife "has dribbled away," and along with the other artifacts of his remote island culture, it is being left to the local museum. The poem ends by evoking a sense of resignation to the frustrations of nostalgia, lamenting Friday's death in an embittered aside that separates their relationship from the inventory of artifacts to emphasize the special poignance of the loss.

CRITICAL VIEWS ON

"Crusoe in England"

BISHOP ON CRUSOE'S RELATION TO FRIDAY

[In the following excerpt from one of Bishop's letters (written April 20, 1974) to her friend and fellow poet James Merrill, she discusses her revision of the crucial passage in which Crusoe describes Friday's arrival.]

No, I am very glad you wrote what you did about "Crusoe [in England]." I don't get much criticism, perhaps because of my gray hairs (or else just nasty remarks, like James Dickey's)—and I'm really grateful. Actually, there was quite a lot more in the last two or three parts of that poem. Then I decided that it was growing boring (this may be one bad effect of giving "readings"—the fear of boring), and that the poem should be speeded up toward the end and not give too many more details—so I cut it quite a lot—the rescue to one line, etc. If I can find the original ms. here (under the ping-pong table, no doubt) I might be able to put back a few lines about Friday. I still like "poor boy"—because he was a lot younger; and because they *couldn't* "communicate" (ghastly word) much. Crusoe guesses at Friday's feelings—but I think you are right and I'll try to restore or add a few lines there before the piece gets to a book. In fact, now that I think of it, I can almost remember 2 or 3 lines after "we were friends"—that's where something is needed, probably.

—Elizabeth Bishop, *One Art* (New York: Farrar, Straus and Giroux, 1994): pp. 584.

HELEN VENDLER ON THE THEME OF DOMESTICITY

[Helen Vendler writes frequently on contemporary poetry and teaches at Harvard University. Her publications include acclaimed studies of Keats, Yeats, George Herbert, Wallace Stevens, and Shakespeare's sonnets in addition to several book-length collections of her reviews and essays. In the following extract, Vendler examines the relationship between domesticity and companionship in "Crusoe in England."]

Elizabeth Bishop's poems in *Geography III* put into relief the continuing vibration of her work between two frequencies—the domestic and the strange. In another poet the alternation might seem a debate, but Bishop drifts rather than divides, gazes rather than chooses. Though the exotic is frequent in her poems of travel, it is not only the exotic that is strange and not only the local that is domestic. (It is more exact to speak, with regard to Bishop, of the domestic rather than the familiar, because what is familiar is always named, in her poetry, in terms of a house, a family, someone beloved, home. And it is truer to speak of the strange rather than of the exotic, because the strange can occur even in the bosom of the familiar, even, most unnervingly, at the domestic hearth.) (. . .)

Domesticity is frail, and it is shaken by the final strangeness of death. Until death, and even after it, the work of domestication of the unfamiliar goes on, all of it a substitute for some assurance of transcendent domesticity, some belief that we are truly, in this world, in our mother's house, that "somebody loves us all." After a loss that destroys one form of domesticity, the effort to reconstitute it in another form begins. The definition of death in certain of Bishop's poems is to have given up on domesticating the world and reestablishing yet once more some form of intimacy. Conversely, the definition of life in the conversion of the strange to the familial, of the unexplored to the knowable, of the alien to the beloved. (. . .)

The whole cycle of domestication and loss can be seen in the long monologue, "Crusoe in England." Crusoe is safely back in England, and his long autobiographical retrospect exposes in full clarity the imperfection of the domestication of nature so long as love is missing, the exhaustion of solitary colonization. (. . .)

Crusoe's efforts at the domestication of nature (making a flute, distilling home brew, even devising a dye out of red berries) create a certain degree of pleasure ("I felt a deep affection for/the smallest of my island industries"), and yet the lack of any society except that of turtles and goats and waterspouts ("sacerdotal beings of glass . . . / Beautiful, yes, but not much company") causes both self-pity and a barely admitted hope. Crusoe, in a metaphysical moment, christens one volcano "*Mont d'Espoir* or *Mount Despair*," mirroring both his desolation and his expectancy. The island landscape has been domesticated, "home-made," and yet domestication can turn to domesticity only with the arrival of Friday: "Just when I thought I couldn't stand it / another minute longer, Friday came." Speechless with joy, Crusoe can speak only in the most vacant and consequently the most comprehensive of words. (. . .)

Love escapes language. Crusoe could describe with the precision of a geographer the exact appearances of volcanoes, turtles, clouds, lava, goats, and waterspouts and waves, but he is reduced to gesture and sketch before the reality of domesticity.

In the final, recapitulatory movement of the poem Bishop first reiterates the conferral of meaning implicit in the domestication of the universe and then contemplates the loss of meaning once the arena of domestication is abandoned.

—Helen Vendler, *Part of Nature, Part of Us: Modern American Poets* (Cambridge: Harvard University Press, 1980): pp. 97, 101, 105–106.

JOANNE FEIT DIEHL ON THE EMERSONIAN SUBLIME

[Joanne Feit Diehl has taught at the University of California, Davis and is the author of *Dickinson and the Romantic Imagination* (1981) and *Women Poets and the American Sublime* (1990). In the extract that follows Diehl sets Bishop in the tradition of the Emersonian Sublime and compares her negotiation of its gender-specific roles to that of Emily Dickinson.]

Separated as she is from Dickinson both by time and temperament, Elizabeth Bishop nonetheless faces an allied if somewhat extenuated version of the Emersonian Sublime, and, once again, the crux of the poetic problem relates to gender. But Bishop, even more than Dickinson, defends against the challenge to her poetic autonomy by ursurping the very terms in which it is made. In other words, Bishop compensates for the recognition of her loss of poetic authority in Emersonian terms by an erasure of the sexual dialectic upon which his vision fundamentally depends. Although Dickinson experiments with a similar strategy, substituting the male for the expected female pronoun or referring to her youthful self as a boy, she moves beyond gender only at intervals; it remains for Bishop to provide a sustained rhetoric of asexuality in order to find an adequate defense against the secondariness to which the American Sublime would sentence her. What distinguishes Bishop's work from the canonical American Sublime, I would suggest, is a loss equivalent to restitution, the enactment of Bishop's "I" as the eye of the traveller or the child, able to recapture an innocence that only apparently evades intimate sexuality or the assertion of gender. One finds in Bishop's poems a map of language where sexuality appears to yield to an asexual self, making possible a poetry that deceptively frees her from the gender-determined role into which she would be cast as a female descendant of the American Sublime. Bishop evades being diminished, exiled, or isolated from the tradition by sidestepping the distinctions imposed by Emerson and his agonistic disciples. Her poems' prevailing absence of the overtly sexual Whitmanian self, the apparent dismissal of heterosexuality, becomes a means of reestablishing woman's unmediated relationship to the world she would make her own. Thus, her poems are a kind of brilliant compensation, a dazzling dismissal of the very distinctions that might otherwise stifle her. (. . .)

The "you" "One Art" fears to lose is not sexually identified, and this identification, of course, makes little difference. But in "Crusoe in England," another poem of loss from the stark territory Bishop called *Geography III*, the issues of same-sex friendship and life on an island, where biological reproduction proves impossible, receive more direct treatment, as Bishop seeks to compensate for Crusoe's severely privative circumstances by the power of an informing eye and the reproductive workings of the fertile imagination. (. . .)

In tones of wry and bitter humor, in language deceptively innocent yet expressive of deep feeling, "Crusoe in England" articulates an extenuating quality which parallels that of Bishop's own poetics. Through the narrative transposition of female to male voice, a voice that describes an asexual world in which the self longs to sustain its imaginative life, Bishop evokes a homoerotic desire equivalent to that which informs her own linguistic imagination. Spoken in the naive tongue of the masculine voyager, what Crusoe's words ironically veil is the plaint of a self questing beyond the hierarchies of the heterosexual, an imagination creating a homeground in exile. Through his conversion of the harshest of geographic regions, Crusoe bizarrely celebrates the powers of the solipsistic imagination transforming the truths of isolation. Although Bishop's carefully modulated ironies and cool reserve distance her from Crusoe's desperate creativity, what her vision shares with her daemonic persona's is a desire to convert such isolation into a region that allows her to reconstitute the relationship between self, words, and world—to identify, solely in her own terms, an island made new for both poetry and friendship. The eye of the traveller and the innocence of the voice combine here to test the wild freedom of privation as well as to acknowledge the pain of its irretrievable loss.

> —Joanne Feit Diehl, "At Home With Loss: Elizabeth Bishop and the American Sublime," *Elizabeth Bishop: Modern Critical Views*, ed. Harold Bloom (New York: Chelsea House, 1985): pp. 178, 180, 182.

STEVEN HAMELMAN ON BISHOP'S RELATION TO DANIEL DEFOE

[Steven Hamelman teaches at the University of South Carolina. In the following extract Hamelman usefully inventories the ways in which Bishop's version of the Crusoe story differ from that of Daniel Defoe's 1719 novel.]

In 1976's dramatic monologue "Crusoe in England," Elizabeth Bishop appropriates the Hero as her persona in order to reconstruct Defoe's character and text in everything but name. The triumphant male equipped with inexhaustible survival skills, domestic proficiency, and imperialistic machismo has been revised into a listless, impotent sex-agenarian. But Bishop does not merely parody the myth of the invincible colonizer; simultaneously, she humanizes Crusoe for our age, our sensibility, by creating a profoundly ambivalent character. (. . .)

Whereas exile causes Bishop's Crusoe to dream about mutilating babies and about islands proliferating toward infinity, Defoe's hero rationalizes his decidedly pleasant imprisonment. Despite his conviction that Providence has chosen to chastise him for earlier sin, he does not stagnate, as his modern counterpart does, devising a "miserable philosophy." Defoe's Crusoe is a doer, Bishop's a thinker, a skeptic. Lacking his predecessor's facile faith, her Crusoe must wrestle with the reason for utter loneliness: "Do I deserve this? I suppose I must. / I wouldn't be here otherwise. Was there / a moment when I actually chose this? / I don't remember, but there could have been." Defoe's Crusoe has neither the time nor the inclination to probe existential cruxes. He blithely, even smugly, depicts his daily life, while Bishop's man frets about living an eternity on islands, "knowing that I had to live / on each and every one, eventually, / for ages, registering their flora, / their fauna, their geography." Here, Bishop implies, is where modern men and woman are stuck—stuck with deadening science and its oppressive detail, paralyzed by the minute intellectual processes they entail, unable to embrace the sensuous fruits and riches of the natural world. Defoe's paradise becomes in Bishop's poem an anachronistic fantasy, an Eden metamorphosed into a post-nuclear wasteland in which the sole human representative articulates all-encompassing bleakness.

Bishop's revision of Friday culminates in the poem's aching last lines: "—And Friday, my dear Friday, died of measles / seventeen years ago come March." By contrast, Defoe's Crusoe seems, at best, patronizingly fond of the native. One of Friday's first lessons is to speak the word "Master"; what follows is servitude to a genial lord. He remains Crusoe's companion until late in the novel when he disappears in Europe after an episode involving wolves. Crusoe ends his tale by itemizing his wealth in England, summarizing his paternal life, and then reminiscing about a return to the island which, contrary to Bishop, has become a thriving colony, presumably with a name. Friday is someone for whom the original Crusoe expresses no regret, no yearning.

Again, if we accept the premise that Bishop is deflating a myth, then her tactics make sense. She elides the original Crusoe's sententiousness, the imperialistic postures, the haughtiness towards Friday, the carnage occurring late in the fiction. Significant, too, is her

Crusoe's statement that "one day they came and took us off." This event has no basis in Defoe's scheme, in which the hero actively plans his departure. Three decades of solitude do not blunt his ambition to deliver himself. No anonymous *they* will take him anywhere, at least not without his consent. He seems to narrate his story from the prow of a ship plunging along the rim of another exotic ocean; he seeks new islands, new mercantile triumphs. The terms "old" and "bored" are unimaginable for him.

But Bishop's Crusoe is old, and he is morally enervated by boredom as he idles away his last years somewhere in England. All the physical, spiritual, emotional, and psychological horrors of exile remain unalleviated. Amenities of civilization, recognition by local authorities, home itself—none of these diminishes his ambivalence and despair in finding meaning nowhere. Being in England or being on his "un-rediscovered, un-renamable" island makes no difference. He dreads each, desires each, confronts emptiness on each.

—Steven Hamelman, "Bishop's 'Crusoe in England,'" *The Explicator* 51, no. 1 (Fall 1992): pp. 51–52.

C.K. DORESKI ON CRUSOE'S CONCERN WITH DOCUMENTATION

[C.K. Doreski is the author of *How to Read and Interpret Poetry* (1988) and *Writing America Black* (1998). In the following extract Doreski analyzes Crusoe's overt concern with language and his inability to articulate his feelings for Friday—a failure that works, paradoxically, to emphasize the intensity and complexity of his emotions.]

From the opening stanza, Bishop is concerned not merely with the boundaries of communication–accounts, registers, books, poems, names, sayings, reading–but with the dependence of all these on social interaction, a human context. What meaning can a name have when there is no one with whom to share its significance? Books previously read show no signs of assisting Crusoe in this island world: "The books / I'd read were full of blanks." All degrees of order seem suspect: Crusoe finds joy and music in his homemade flute in spite of its weird scale, but he relinquishes his hold on language; words belong elsewhere.

The cacophony of *baa, shriek, hiss* reiterates the unimportance of embellished utterance. On this island, necessity dictates: The gut speaks. Yet Crusoe yearns for reciprocity. His insularity prompts a malignant introversion; dreams play off his daylight fears. Soon he understands his solitary state in the human enterprise as not merely a term of exile, but forever.

The ultimate erasure of language occurs at the moment of intimate resolution of the state of exile:

> Just when I thought I couldn't stand it
> another minute longer, Friday came.
> (Accounts of that have everything all wrong.)

After the nightmarish threat of intellectual pedantry throughout eternity, Crusoe surrenders his civilization. His need for contact with his own kind confounds his emotional grasp of the state of exile. Ordinary language, the language of accounts, cannot grasp the utter disruption of Crusoe's established emotional state triggered by the direct physical confrontation with a healthy otherness; in retrospect, unable to conjure a more emotive language, Crusoe can only confess that

> Friday was nice.
> Friday was nice, and we were friends.

Yet the effect of this apparent failure of rhetorical prowess is to reiterate the original emotional value of these simple words. If language preserved itself for occasions of significance (as this encounter suggests), the apparent numbness of the cliché dissipates. With casual, offhand language, Bishop deliberately cloaks the interiority of this relationship. Unlike Defoe, who immediately establishes Crusoe and Friday as a hierarchical master-servant relationship, Bishop fosters the immediate equality of friendship. She has chosen to approximate the "infant sight" of original relationship with these deliberately disposable words, but in doing so she raises the issue of dramatic plausibility. Can it be that the Crusoe who is so able to recount and register his world and experiences alone is unable to articulate beyond these vague utterances the details of his saving relationship with Friday? Or is the subtle linguistic argument intended to be his own?

—C.K. Doreski, *Elizabeth Bishop: The Restraints of Language* (New York: Oxford University Press, 1993): pp. 132–133.

[Susan McCabe is an assistant professor at Arizona State University and is the author of *Elizabeth Bishop: Her Poetics of Loss* (1994). In the following extract McCabe discusses parallels between "Crusoe in England" and Bishop's life-story in order to examine her reasons for transforming Defoe's novel of adventure into an elegiac poem.]

When Bishop drafts the poem in 1964, she feels perhaps her most liminal in her home with Lota: it is the year before she accepts a teaching job at the University of Washington, the year Lota's emotional and physical health is deteriorating after extensive involvement in Brazilian politics. In 1967 Lota reunites with Bishop in New York and dies of an overdose of Valium, after, in Bishop's words, "at least 13 happy years with her, the happiest of [her] life" (*One Art* 470). When she returns to Brazil to reclaim her recently purchased Ouro Prêto home, she is treated poorly by her Brazilian neighbors, who blame her and make her into a "scapegoat," as she puts it in a letter (. . .)

Exile—Return—Exile: the emotional map of "Crusoe" that speaks for an otherness only the redispossessed can know (Crusoe and Friday now become interchangeable possible identifications for her).(. . .)

Both Bishop's home in Brazil and her loss of it make her live with a necessary distance from objects and landscape so that she never hopes to claim them fully. Things, of so much value to Defoe's Crusoe, become quite explicitly nothing. The last stanza refuses cultural consumption, the making of lived experience into museum artifact, inevitably epitaphic and disembodied: (. . .)

"The memory of the time" is kept into the future ("come March") by Friday, whose death inscribed after a catalogue of things, forbids the making of him into artifact. The parasol "will work" (usable even if it can't protect), but out of its context of exiled homemaking, without the communion with an other, it turns into dead nature. The disinvested poet challenges, "How can anyone want such things?"

Bishop is always somewhat suspicious of objects, and especially in "Crusoe" they become porous emblems of perishability.

The objects in "Crusoe" have been only vital as they have lived in their active, present tense, in their "remembering" as an act of creation, and perhaps, only becoming animate with the gaze and "living soul" offered by the other. I am not suggesting that Bishop denies art any potency; it is just that she is radically redefining it in terms of her losses, necessarily converting an adventure into an elegy. Significantly, Bishop is both reaching her height as a poet (*Geography III* is arguably her best volume) and giving up her "art," at least in the senses of art as mastery or as possession. Pragmatic utility founders without imaginative enactment or emotional fulfillment. After being asked to leave the house of Petropolis in 1966 under the advice of Lota's psychiatrist, Bishop makes a catalogue of what is left over from her ship-wrecked relationship into a draft called "Inventory": "'out in half an hour,' 'after fifteen years with a few dirty clothes in a busted suitcase, no home any more, no claim (legally) to anything here" (Millier 384). Things lose their borders for the disenfranchised lover.

—Susan McCabe, "Bishop in Brazil: Writing the Un-renamable," *Women Poets of the Americas: Toward a Pan-American Gathering* (Notre Dame: University of Notre Dame Press, 1999): pp. 86, 190–192.

"The End of March"

"The End of March" appeared in *Geography III* (1976), Bishop's final collection, a book that both recapitulates and extends the meditations and explorations begun in earlier volumes. Thus the "crooked box/set up on pilings" in the poem recalls the weathered wooden structure of "The Monument," also a seaside shelter, even as the questioning speaker of the later poem echoes the skeptical second voice of the earlier one. "The End of March" recounts a journey out and back along a Duxbury beach toward an abandoned house that the speaker has seen on other walks and dreams of retiring to. The house represents an ideal of withdrawal from the imperative to use time productively: "I'd like to retire there and do *nothing*," the speaker emphatically declares. But this fantasy of self-isolation proves "impossible" to realize, just as the house, which is "boarded up" anyway, proves too far to walk to on such a cold day. The poem's questions, qualifications, parenthetical asides, and second-guesses evoke a sense of uncertainty and incompleteness, and in a way the poem can be seen as a draft of itself—an effect appropriate to its focus on a hypothetical state of self-sufficiency and fulfillment. The poem opens by providing a description of the harsh conditions under which the speaker and her fellow travelers make their journey. It is "scarcely the day/to take a walk on that long beach" due to the cold temperature and the wind. The tide is low and the ocean seems "shrunken," conditions that increase the sense of desolation and emphasize the power of the elements even as they introduce an idea of withdrawal that is central to the dream-house ideal elaborated in the poem. Nature is presented in its disorderliness rather than as a subtly harmonious whole: not only are the walkers self-admittedly out of place, but nature's own patterns are "disrupted." The "lone flight of Canada geese" are out of "formation" even as the surf is blown back into a "steely mist."

The poem's emphatic fidelity to the experience of the walk emerges in the way it catalogues objects and images which meaning seems to have deserted, objects that resist absorption into larger framing narratives. Curiously, the sky is "darker" than the water, just as the size of the dog-prints makes them seem "more like lion-prints." The lengths of wet white string," another of the scene's eccentricities, prove similarly inexplicable, ending in a "thick white snarl" that resembles a "sodden ghost." The speaker sifts among possible contexts for what she observes during the walk, but her speculations remain inconclusive—a pattern she underlines at the end of the stanza with an image of another loose end she doesn't tie up: "A kite string?—But no kite."

The enumeration of dubious details shifts into a description of a similarly "dubious" dream-house. Just as the poem can be viewed as its own rough draft in light of its prosy style, so the "proto-dream-house" is construed as a model of itself. It is also a "crypto-dream-house": the prefix "crypto" evokes the idea of a tomb (an association her plan for doing "*nothing*" in it bears out) even as it reinforces the idea of its obscurity, as if, like notes for a poem, it still needed to be deciphered or made sense of. The dream-life housed within it is sketched out as a respite from productivity of a literary kind: doing "*nothing*, or nothing much" means doing all the things preparatory to writing poems, but without the finished product: making observations, reading, writing "useless notes."

The description of a fantasized retirement shifts course as the speaker takes stock of the accommodations. Since "there *is* a chimney" the speaker concludes that there "must be a stove," and a wire that connects the house to "something off behind the dunes" suggests the house features electrical power. Much like what she observes on the beach earlier in the poem, the house invites the speaker to do some guesswork. Not only is the house engaged on the same qualified, uncertain terms as the beachscape, but its "possibly" electrical wire recalls what is "possibly" a kite string in the second stanza: both images evoke a notion of disconnection that reinforces the themes of withdrawal and isolation embodied in the speaker's dream-house retirement. Though the house seems "perfect," retirement to it is "impossible" even as the house itself is unreachable and impenetrable: the wind was "much too cold" that day "even to get that far,/and of course the house was boarded up."

The last stanza of the poem recounts the return journey and is itself a return from a preoccupation with an imagined existence to the mode of observation exhibited in the earlier stanzas, in which vision is guided principally by the contents and contours of the land-scape itself. The momentary appearance of the sun transforms the scene, and for "just a minute" the "drab, damp, scattered stones" become "multi-colored." The late-afternoon sun throws "long shad-ows" off some of the stones, which "pull them in again" when it goes in, a rapid, contradictory-seeming phenomenon that prompts the speaker to fictionalize it as a "teasing" gesture. Earlier in the poem the acknowledgement that there is "no kite" diminishes the possibil-ity that what the speaker happens upon is "kite string," and in much the same way her initial reaction to her idea that the stones are "teas-ing the lion sun" is to discount it by remarking the sun's position "behind them." But in the last stanza this skeptical impulse yields in turn not to a dream withdrawal but to a comprehensive fiction of connection. The enigmas of the second stanza—the dog-prints "so big/they were more like lion-prints" and "endless" lengths of unat-tached string—are woven together into an orderly text: "those big, majestic paw-prints" are the tracks, by this whimsical account, of the "lion sun," while the tangled string is left over from a kite the sun "batted. . . out of the sky to play with."

"The End of March"

BISHOP ON ART AND THE UNCONSCIOUS

[The following passage is excerpted from Bishop's famous letter to Anne Stevenson, in which she describes her views on the
relation between art and the unconscious before going on to
suggest that appreciating art, like creating it, requires a "perfectly useless concentration"—an idea that resonates with her
interest in retiring to her dream-house and doing "nothing
much" in "The End of March."]

There is no "split" [between the role of consciousness and sub-con-
sciousness in art]. Dreams, works of art (some) glimpses of the
always-more-successful surrealism of everyday life, unexpected
moments of empathy (is it?), catch a peripheral vision of whatever it
is one can never really see full-face but that seems enormously
important. I can't believe we are wholly irrational—and I do admire
Darwin—But reading Darwin one admires the beautiful solid case
being built up out of his endless, heroic observations, almost unconscious or automatic—and then comes a sudden relaxation, a forget-
ful phrase, and one feels that strangeness of his undertaking, sees the
lonely young man, his eyes fixed on facts and minute details, sink-
ing or sliding giddily off into the unknown. What one seems to want
in art, in experiencing it, is the same thing that is necessary for its
creation, a self-forgetful, perfectly useless concentration.

> —Elizabeth Bishop, letter to Anne Stevenson, *Elizabeth Bishop* (New
> York: Twayne, 1966): pp. 66. Reprinted in *Elizabeth Bishop and Her
> Art*, ed. Lloyd Schwartz and Sybil Estess (Ann Arbor: University of
> Michigan Press, 1983): pp. 228.

PENELOPE LAURANS ON BISHOP'S PROSODY

[Penelope Laurans has worked as an editor for the *Yale Review*
and is currently Associate Dean of Yale College. In the following extract, Laurans examines Bishop's prosody and in

particular her tendency, as in "The End of March," to use prose rhythms as a way of limiting the articulation of heightened emotions.]

It is consistent with Bishop's own preference for the natural that, in her poems, form always yields to the exigency of what she is trying to say. Her patterns are a result of her insistence that formal structures adapt to the developing progression of the poem, rather than predetermine that progression. Of course no good poet allows form to dictate what he is going to say. But many will let it guide them in making choices. Bishop, however, rarely seems to permit this to happen. (. . .)

Thematically, Bishop's poetry tends toward Romantic subject matter problems of isolation, of loss, of the quest for union with something beyond the self, press with dramatic force in her work. These highly charged questions, however, are nearly always countered by the way they are presented, which has earned for the tone of her verse such critical characterizations as "matter-of-fact and understated" and "flat and modest." Indeed, it seems to me that Bishop exercises her technical proficiency to cut her poetry off from any of that "spontaneous overflow of powerful feeling" so immediately central to the Romantic imagination. Frequently it is this quality of restraint that keeps the poetry from sentimental excess and gives it its elegantly muted, modernist quality. (. . .)

In a poem like "The End of March," one is able to see how reluctant Bishop is to allow technical intensity and thematic passion to correspond in her work. She parcels out her poem's appeal to the reader's emotions charily, using prose passages to contradict what she expressly states, and lyric passages to imply what she is disinclined to make plain. (. . .)

While the words say one thing, the metrical impulse of the poem communicates precisely the opposite to the reader. The passage in which Bishop describes the house and her wish to reach it contains far and away the most neutral, prose-like writing of the poem: (. . .)

Everything in the diction and movement of the verse here—its ordinariness, its prosy, conversational sound and flow, as if Bishop were simply talking to the reader—works to diminish the excitement of the ideal she is imagining. Here is the "naturalness" Bishop likes, with a vengeance.

There is real verbal and metrical excitement in this poem, however, at its conclusion: (. . .)

The dynamic way in which Bishop allows these lines to swing into a kind of lyric movement that is often rationed in her poetry shows that this is an energy Bishop values too much to make the other, more passive state her permanent ideal, no matter what she says directly. In fact, the final five lines of the poem make their own small, passionately lyrical stanza—two lines of pentameter, interspersed with two four stress lines, and completed by a long six stress line. Their climactic movement works to persuade the reader that, while Bishop says she longs for a rickety house on a hill, what she actually values is the large, dangerous universe where "all the untidy activity continues, / awful but cheerful."

The point here is that Bishop's daydream—the thing she says, however whimsically and momentarily, she desires—is described in the most flat, dead-pan verse, while a deeper, unspoken ideal is conveyed by the later momentum of the poetry. Significantly, Bishop releases her poem lyrically only at a moment which is not explicitly its thematic high point. Of course this moment becomes its high point, but that is another matter. The important fact is that Bishop seems reluctant to allow metrical intensity and plain-spokenness to correspond, as if she were afraid that the one might spoil or cheapen the other.

—Penelope Laurans, "'Old Correspondences': Prosodic Transformations in Elizabeth Bishop," *Elizabeth Bishop and Her Art* (Ann Arbor: University of Michigan Press, 1983): pp. 76, 90–93.

SHEROD SANTOS ON BISHOP'S PATIENCE

[Sherod Santos teaches at the University of Missouri and is the author of several collections of poetry, including *Accidental Weather* (1982), *City of Women* (1993), and *Pilot Star Elegies* (1999). In this extract Santos discusses how Bishop's characteristic patience and qualified style work to sponsor the illusion of seeing into the "inner workings" of a poem like "The End of March."]

"The End of March," one of the later poems out of *Geography III*, may not belong in the canon of great Elizabeth Bishop poems, but perhaps that makes it all the more interesting to consider (and the canon all that more amazing to regard) since it still gives such obvious proof of what has become, to my mind anyway, the great secret gift Bishop left behind: her enormous and indefatigable *Patience*. (. . .)

It is a principle of physics that when matter is compressed it becomes more volatile, and it's a similar principle that seems to govern Pound's notion of the image. Through a process of intense concentration on some particular detail, the detail itself taken on a kind of heightened energy it wouldn't ordinarily have. In terms of time, that concentration is achieved by hurrying things up, by accelerating the pace of the poem—the emotional complex caught in an *instant* of time. Bishop's poems, on the other hand, make use of an entirely different conception of time. The method seems almost to be in the *waiting*, in allowing the imagination to *linger*, in the feeling that the eye can *take its own sweet time*. The process at last becomes as important to the poem as the thing which set the process in motion. One of the things that happens as a result is that the poet's own intuitive responses to the world become just another series of things within the world. And the instant of revelation—a phrase, I'm sure, Bishop would not have felt comfortable with—that instant gives way to an ongoing contemplation. As Bishop explains it in her own aside from "Poem":" 'visions' is / too serious a word—our looks."

In one sense, what Bishop has done is demystify the poet by exposing the inner workings of the poem. It is an effect that's similar, I would guess, to that created by a magician who, while performing his illusions, keeps telling the audience how he creates those illusions: you might be just as fascinated by the illusions themselves, but you would no longer be able to pretend they were magic. (. . .)

One can see how, by simply speeding up or compressing the stanza, the poet appears more clearly the source of the image, the magician pretending to his imaginary powers. But in Bishop's version we are given the process as well, we are shown how the image arrived quite naturally from a complex of forces in the world itself (though perhaps that too is just another illusion). The poet's role is now a more modest one, and the accumulation of fairly predictable adjectives—"drab," "damp," "scattered," "multi-colored," "long," "individual"—those words only serve to make the whole event seem that much more commonplace, that much less magical.

Bishop's sense of reserve, both in and out of her work, is famous by now, and it's perhaps just that reserve which makes so loveable the abundance of those characteristic little asides in her poems, those moments when she suddenly and rather merrily (a little like Hitchcock) pops up out of nowhere and corrects her first perception, or readjusts the focus a little, or asks a question, or just for the hell of it takes a bow. (. . .)

"The End of March" is one of the rare poems in which Bishop actually appears as a "character," and that third stanza has always seemed to me as close to a self-portrait as we're likely to get from her. But look at what that stanza is about. In a way that Robert Bly's famous little poem "Watering the Horse" never really is, this poem is about "giving up all ambition." In Bly's poem the idea is proclaimed so boastfully one suspects it couldn't be true; in Bishop's it's made so seductive one fears it is.

—Sherod Santos, "The End of March," *Field* 31 (Fall 1984): pp. 29–32.

LORRIE GOLDENSOHN ON RENUNCIATION IN *GEOGRAPHY III*

[Lorrie Goldensohn teaches at Vassar College and is the author of *Dreamwork* (1980), a collection of poems, and *Elizabeth Bishop: The Biography of a Poetry* (1992), from which the following extract is drawn. Goldensohn compares the speaker's renunciation of her dream of retirement to similar movements in several other poems from *Geography III*.]

In "One Art," "Loved houses" and "lovely cities" have both disappeared; in "The End of March," after a cold walk along the beach, where "Everything was as withdrawn as possible," the "proto-dream house,/my crypto-dream house" is boarded up. No more than

Crusoe's actual, returned-to England, the dream house won't do. We wanted to get to the house, our empty paradise, but we couldn't. First our faces froze on the one side, then the other. On this trip, as for the passenger of "Night City," for Crusoe, and for the Boston traveler of "The Moose," there isn't any homecoming. The dream of ultimate satisfaction stays remote, just as urban reality or inaccessible pastness closes out the other voyagers from return. Nevertheless, the poem ends on the positive exposure played out between the tide, the "lion sun," and the bezeled stones set "high enough," and the contents of satisfaction are changing subtly.

The goal of the roundtripper, the proto-dream house, has many things about it that seem as unlivably "dubious" as the forbidding climate of "Night City" or the poet's desk in "12 O'Clock News." If we look at the modifiers for the dream house, moving from proto to cryptic to dubious, something interesting emerges in that devaluing sequence, pulling together all the protagonists of the book in a common dilemma with a common solution. Just as the little girl in the waiting room is yanked back into history, and Crusoe is made to face England, and the master loser practices the terminations of her one art, writing, the hiker in "The End Of March" seems compelled to yield up her fondness for "dubious" and "impossible" dream houses. The renunciation of this dream house might constitute a denial of what the poet recognizes as dangerous solitude, possibly wrapped in alcoholic haze. The poem explores the possibility of this denial, as it fingers the lovely, seductive aloneness it proposes and then dismisses: (. . .)

The alcohol-fuddled Edwin Boomer, the Prisoner, all of the looking-glass proto-selves that dreamt of such houses are wryly being put aside. Bishop also redirects a style as well as a subject: twice in this poem there are moments that invite the fantastic personae that bloomed in her early work as Man-moth, weed, sandpiper, Giant Toad, and so on; but in this late poem the cluster of feeling and insight that would have urged the creation of such beings flames up suggestively, "diaphanously," and then like gas from that rejected stove turns down, subject to other controls. (. . .)

Very lightly, it seems to me, one is being nudged by Bishop to look more steadily at her world of poem-making, and to consider her place as artist, as place in this metaphoric sense begins to substitute for Bishop's more usual literal preoccupation with geography. At the close of her career, as "One Art" indicates, she must "practice losing farther, losing faster:/places and names, and where it was you meant/ to travel." In *Geography III*, Bishop settles at least partially for a home in the exercise of her art, harnessed alongside others of her kind.

—Lorrie Goldensohn, *Elizabeth Bishop: The Biography of a Poetry* (New York: Columbia University Press, 1992): pp. 262–264.

JOHN HOLLANDER REVIEWS *GEOGRAPHY III*

[John Hollander, prize-winning poet and distinguished critic, currently teaches at Yale University. He is the author of numerous collections of poetry, including *The Night Mirror* (1971), *Powers of Thirteen* (1983), and *Tesserae and Other Poems* (1993). His critical works include *The Figure of Echo* (1981), *Rhyme's Reason* (1981), and *The Work of Poetry* (1997), from which the following extract is drawn. Hollander situates *Geography III* within the context of Bishop's previous books and suggests its virtues derive in part from its imaginative engagement with her prior poetic accomplishments.]

Geography III is a magnificent book of ten poems whose power and beauty would make it seem gross to ask for more of them. Its epigraph is a catechistic geography lesson quoted from a nineteenth-century textbook, claimed for parable in that seamless way of allowing picture to run into image that the poet made her own. In this instance, it is by her own added italicized questions about mapped bodies—of land, of water—and about direction, following the epigraph in its own language but now become fully figurative. The opening poem of Bishop's first volume, *North & South*, is called "The Map"; in all the work that followed it, the poet was concerned with mappings of the possible world. More generally, she had pursued the ways in which pictures, models, representations of all sorts begin to take on lives of their own under the generative force of that analogue of loves between persons that moves between nature and consciousness. We might, somewhat lamely, call it passionate attention. Its caresses, extended by awareness that pulses with imagination, are not only those of the eye and ear at moments of privileged experience, but rather at the times of composition, of representing anew. The mapmakers' colors, "more delicate than the historians'," are as much part of a larger, general Nature as are the raw particulars of unrepresented sea and sky, tree and hill, street and storefront, roof and watertank. Much of the praise given Bishop's work has directed itself to her command of observation, the focus of her vision, the unmannered quality of her rhetoric—almost as if she were a novelist, and almost as if love of life could only be manifested in the accuracy and interestingness of one's accounts of the shapes that human activity casts on nature.

But the passionate attention does not reveal itself in reportage. Love remains one of its principal tropes, just as the reading, interpreting, and reconstituting of nature in one's poems remains a model of what love may be and do. The representations–the charts, pictures, structures, dreams, and fables of memory–that one makes are themselves the geographies that, in our later sense of the word, they map and annotate. The radical invention of a figurative geography in *North & South*, the mapping of personal history implicit there, are perhaps Bishop's *Geography I*; after the Nova Scotian scenes and urban landscapes to the south of them in *A Cold Spring*, lit and shaded by love and loss, the grouped Brazilian poems and memories, rediscoveries even, of childhood yet further to the north, asked questions of travel. A literal geographic distinction, a north and south of then and now, gained new mythopoetic force; all that intensely and chastely observed material could only have become more than very, very good writing when it got poetically compounded with the figurative geography books of her earlier poems. *Questions of Travel* is thus, perhaps, her *Geography II*.

This book is a third, by title and by design, and, by its mode of recapitulation; a review of the previous two courses as well as an advanced text. Like all major poetry, it both demands prerequisites and invites the new student, and each of these to far greater degrees than most of the casual verse we still call poetry can ever do. The important poems here seem to me to derive their immense power from the energies of the poet's creative present and from the richness and stead-fastness of her created past ("A yesterday I find almost impossible to lift," she allows in the last line of the last poem in the book). Yes, if yesterdays are to be carried as burdens, one would agree; but even yesteryears can themselves, if one is imaginatively fortunate, become monuments to be climbed, to be looked about and even ahead from, to be questioned and pondered themselves.

—John Hollander, *The Work of Poetry* (New York: Columbia University Press, 1997): pp. 280–281.

LANGDON HAMMER RELATES BISHOP'S POEMS TO HER LETTERS

[Langdon Hammer is the author of *Hart Crane and Allen Tate: Janus-Faced Modernism* (1993), and he co-edited a selection of Crane's letters with Brom Weber. He teaches at Yale University. In the following extract Hammer discusses Bishop's idealization of unproductiveness in "The End of March" and her famous "Darwin letter." He goes on to suggest that the poet's correspondence models an idea of "useless" literary work that both the style and themes of her poetry reflect.]

The epigraph for this essay, which comes from a letter Bishop wrote to Anne Stevenson (one of several important well-known letters not included in *One Art*), is a statement about the general purpose of art: "What one seems to want in art, in experiencing it, is the same thing that is necessary for its creation, a self-forgetful, perfectly useless concentration" (Schwartz and Estess 288). This "useless concentration" is partaken of equally by people who create art and people who experience it, whose roles Bishop sees as exchangeable, like those of writer and reader in the personal letter. It is a "self-forgetful" concentration because in this state one's attention is absorbed by an object outside the self; to enter it is to enter the liminal, "potential space" Winnicott speaks of, a space of reverie where the subject is "held" by an object. Bishop's model of art is mimetic to the extent that her ideal artist is a copyist, the describer of a world of objects. In fact, the artist Bishop mentions in her letter to Stevenson is a scientist, Darwin. But truth to objects is not the final concern of this art.

Rather, the artist's relation to the world is the ground for an inter-subjective relation—an intimacy—between artist and audience. (. . .)

The state of "useless concentration" entails for Bishop an inward turning, a wish for withdrawal that is more embattled and aggressive than accounts of Bishop's rhetorical restraint have so far allowed. In *Geography III* (1976), Bishop's last and shortest book, where "Poem" appears, that wish is persistent and explicit. For example, in the middle section of "The End of March," the poet recalls a cold walk along the ocean with an unspecified companion or compan-ions, having as her goal a house she had seen on other walks: (. . .)

There is indeed a kind of vengeance, a hostility toward literary work and the institutions of literary culture, expressed in Bishop's longing for the dream house. (. . .)

The "third area," Winnicott's "potential space," is set apart from the world by a "frame" in a way that allows "contemplative," rather than "expedient," end-directed activity to take place (Milner 80–81). Among the many images of such an enclosure in Bishop's writing, the dream house in "The End of March" is the most important. The contemplation, the "useless concentration" it permits is a willful negation of the social imperative to do productive work, which was always defined, for Bishop as for her peers, by the criteria of *quantity and scale* (. . .)

Unlike Lowell, Bishop does not wish for "a long stretch of noth-ing but work." Bishop's wish (which is opposed even to what she is doing as she writes these lines) is to give up working, "to retire" to the dream house "and do *nothing.*" Yet this "nothing" is something to be achieved, the special product Bishop dreams of producing, an impossible substance like the heavy light suspended in a droplet on the windowpane.

Doing "nothing," then, does not mean being inactive. It means doing "nothing much": reading books that are too long and boring to finish, writing "useless notes." As in correspondence, reading and writing are seen here as two forms of a single activity that is solitary and "self-forgetful" at once. And the books Bishop dreams of read-ing are "boring" in the way that correspondence usually is, includ-ing the long book of Bishop's own letters. (. . .)

That the dream house turns out to be a "perfect! But—impossible" place (*Poems* 180) does not, however, cancel the desires sheltered there; it confines the articulation of those desires to a wish, the fulfillment of which remains a dream. The reading and writing that Bishop dreams of doing in the house are fantasy forms of the "useless," nonproductive literary activity toward which, in her ordinary life, Bishop's letter writing aspired. I have argued that correspondence is the model for an imaginative ideal Bishop sought to realize in poetry, and that her poems can be understood as a certain kind of letter. But Bishop's letters themselves only point to such an ideal. They do not escape the oppositions that structure Bishop's conflicted experience of work, including the generic distinction between poems and letters.

—Langdon Hammer, "Useless Concentration: Life and Work in Elizabeth Bishop's Letters and Poems," *American Literary History* 9, no. 1 (Spring 1997): pp. 175–178.

WORKS BY

Elizabeth Bishop

North and South. 1946.

Poems: North and South—A Cold Spring. 1955.

The Diary of "Helena Morley." 1957.

Brazil. 1962.

Questions of Travel. 1965.

The Complete Poems. 1969.

Geography III. 1976

The Complete Poems 1927–1979. 1983.

The Collected Prose. 1984.

One Art. 1994.

Elizabeth Bishop

Bloom, Harold. ed. *Elizabeth Bishop*. New York: Chelsea House, 1985.

Brogan, Jacqueline V. "Elizabeth Bishop: Perversity as Voice." *American Poetry 7*, no. 2 (Winter 1990): pp. 31–49.

Bromwich, David. *Skeptical Music*. Chicago: University of Chicago Press, 2001.

Brown, Ashley. "Elizabeth Bishop in Brazil." *Southern Review*, October, 1977.

Colwell, Anne. *Inscrutable Houses: Metaphors of the Body in the Poems of Elizabeth Bishop*. Tuscaloosa: University of Alabama Press, 1997.

Costello, Bonnie. *Elizabeth Bishop: Questions of Mastery*. Cambridge: Harvard University Press, 1991.

Dickie, Margaret. "Seeing is Re-seeing: Sylvia Plath and Elizabeth Bishop." *American Literature 65*, no. 1 (March 1993): pp. 131–146.

Diehl, Joanne Feit. *Elizabeth Bishop and Marianne Moore: The Psychodynamics of Creativity*. Princeton University Press, 1993.

Dodd, Elizabeth. *The Veiled Mirror and the Woman Poet: H.D., Louise Bogan, Elizabeth Bishop, and Louise Gluck*. Columbia: University of Missouri Press, 1992.

Doreski, C.K. *Elizabeth Bishop: The Restraints of Language*. New York: Oxford University Press, 1993.

Erkkila, Betsy. "Elizabeth Bishop, Modernism, and the Left." *American Literary History 8*, no. 2 (Summer 1996): pp. 284–310.

Goldensohn, Lorrie. *Elizabeth Bishop: The Biography of a Poetry*. New York: Columbia University Press, 1992.

Green, Fiona. "Locating the Lyric: Marianne Moore, Elizabeth Bishop and the Second World War." *Locations of Literary Modernism*. ed. Alex Davis and Lee Jenkins. Cambridge: Cambridge University Press, 2000.

Hamelman, Steven. "Bishop's 'Crusoe in England.'" *The Explicator 51*, no. 1 (Fall 1992): pp. 50–53.

Hammer, Langdon. "Useless Concentration: Life and Work in Elizabeth Bishop's Letters And Poems." *American Literary History 9*, no. 1 (Spring 1997): pp. 162–178.

———. "The New Elizabeth Bishop." *Yale Review 82*, no. 2 (1994): pp. 135–149.

Handa, Carolyn. "Vision and Change: The Poetry of Elizabeth Bishop." *America Poetry 3*, no. 2 (Winter 1986): pp. 18–34.

Harrison, Victoria. *Elizabeth Bishop's Poetics of Intimacy*. Cambridge: Cambridge University Press, 1993.

Heaney, Seamus. *The Redress of Poetry*. New York: Farrar, Straus and Giroux, 1995.

Hollander, John. *The Work of Poetry*. New York: Columbia University Press, 1997.

Jarraway, David R. "'O Canada!': The Spectral Lesbian Poetics of Elizabeth Bishop." *PMLA 113*, no. 2 (March 1998): pp. 243–58.

Kalstone, David. *Becoming a Poet: Elizabeth Bishop with Marianne Moore and Robert Lowell*. New York: Farrar, Straus and Giroux, 1989.

———. *Five Temperments*. New York: Oxford University Press, 1977.

Lombardi, Marilyn May. ed. *Elizabeth Bishop: The Geography of Gender*. Charlottesville: University Press of Virginia, 1993.

Longenbach, James. "Elizabeth Bishop's Social Conscience." *ELH 62* (1995): pp. 468–483.

———. "Elizabeth Bishop and the Story of Postmodernism." *Southern Review 28*, no. 3 (Summer 1992): pp. 469–484.

Lowell, Robert, *Sewanee Review 55* (Summer 1947): pp. 497–499.

Mazzaro, Jerome. *Postmodern American Poetry*. Urbana: University of Illinois Press, 1980.

McCabe, Susan. *Elizabeth Bishop: Her Poetics of Loss*. University Park: Pennsylvania State University Press, 1994.

Merrin, Jeredith. *An Enabling Humility: Marianne Moore, Elizabeth Bishop, and the Uses of Tradition*. New Brunswick: Rutgers University Press, 1990.

Millier, Brett C. *Elizabeth Bishop: Life and the Memory of It.* Berkeley: University of California Press, 1993.

Newman, Anne R. "Elizabeth Bishop's 'Roosters.'" *Pebble: A Book of Rereadings in Recent American Poetry.* ed. Greg Kuzma. Lincoln, NE: The Best Cellar Press, 1979.

Page, Barbara. "The Rising Figure of the Poet: Elizabeth Bishop in Letters and Biography." *Contemporary Literature 37*, no. 1 (Spring 1996): pp. 119–131.

Parker, Robert Dale. *The Unbeliever: The Poetry of Elizabeth Bishop.* Urbana: University of Illinois Press, 1988.

Procopiow, Norma. "Survival Kit: The Poetry of Elizabeth Bishop." *Centennial Review 25*, no. 1 (Winter 1981): pp. 1–19.

Rotella, Guy. *Reading and Writing Nature: The Poetry of Robert Frost, Wallace Stevens, Marianne Moore, and Elizabeth Bishop.* Boston: Northeastern University Press, 1991.

Santos, Sherod. "The End of March." *Field 31* (Fall 1984): pp. 29–32.

Schwartz, Lloyd, and Sybil P. Estess. eds. *Elizabeth Bishop and Her Art.* Ann Arbor: University of Michigan Press, 1983.

Shetley, Vernon. "On Elizabeth Bishop." *Raritan 14*, no. 3 (Winter 1995): pp. 151–163.

Spiegelman, Willard. "Elizabeth Bishop's 'Natural Heroism.'" *Centennial Review 22*, no. 7 (Winter 1978): pp. 28–44.

Spires, Elizabeth. "Questions of Knowledge." *Field 31* (Fall 1984): pp. 20–23.

Stevenson, Anne. *Elizabeth Bishop.* New York: Twayne, 1966.

Travisano, Thomas. "The Elizabeth Bishop Phenomenon." *New Literary History 26*, no. 4 (Fall 1995): pp. 903–930.

Vendler, Helen. *Part of Nature, Part of Us: Modern American Poets.* Cambridge: Harvard University Press, 1980.

———. "The Poems of Elizabeth Bishop." *Critical Inquiry 13*, no. 4 (Summer 1987): pp. 825–838.

Wallace, Patricia. "Erasing the Maternal: Rereading Elizabeth Bishop." *Iowa Review 22*, no. 2 (Spring-Summer 1992): pp. 82–103.

Wolosky, Shira. "Representing Other Voices: Rhetorical Perspective in Elizabeth Bishop." *Style 29*, no. 1 (Spring 1995): pp. 1–17.

ACKNOWLEDGMENTS

"Thomas, Bishop, and Williams" by Robert Lowell. First published in the Sewanee Review, vol. 55, no. 3, 1947 © 1974 by the University of the South. Reprinted with the Permission of the editor.

Reprinted by permission of the publisher from *Elizabeth Bishop: Questions of Mastery* by Bonnie Costello, Cambridge, Mass.: Harvard University Press, pp. 109, 115-116, 218-219, Copyright © 1991 by the President and the Fellows of Harvard College.

The Redress of Poetry by Seamus Heaney © 1995 by Farrar, Straus, and Giroux. Reprinted by Permission.

The Body and the Song: Elizabeth Bishop's Poetics by Marilyn May Lombardi. © 1995 by the Board of Trustees, Southern Illinois University, reproduced by the Permission of the publisher.

Skeptical Music by David Bromwich © 2001 by University of Chicago Press. Reprinted by Permission.

One Art, ed. Robert Giroux © 1994 by Farrar, Straus and Giroux. Reprinted by Permission.

Review of *North and South* by Louise Bogan from *The New Yorker* (October 5, 1946). Reprinted in *Elizabeth Bishop and Her Art,* ed. Lloyd Schwartz and Sybil Estess © 1983 by the University of Michigan Press. Reprinted by Permission.

"Elizabeth Bishop's 'Natural Heroism,'" by Willard Spiegelman. © 1978 from *Centennial Review 22,* no.1, by Michigan State University Press. Reprinted by Permission.

Elizabeth Bishop's Poetics of Intimacy by Victoria Harrison © 1993 by Cambridge University Press. Reprinted with the Permission of Cambridge University Press.

Longenbach, James. Elizabeth Bishop's Social Conscience. English Literary 62 (1995), 468-469. © The John Hopkins University Press. Reprinted by Permission of the John Hopkins University Press.

"Conjuring With Nature" by David Kalstone © 1971 from *Twentieth-Century Literature in Retrospect* by Harvard University Press. Reprinted by Permission.

"Questions of Knowledge" by Elizabeth Spires © 1984 from *Field*, 31. Reprinted by Permission.

INDEX OF
Themes and Ideas